WHAT PEOPLE ARE SAYING

"An important work. Ann Arnold's effort to both tell the tale of her family's survival during the Holocaust while being a part of encouraging the next generation to embrace tolerance is inspiring."

— Michael Cohen
Eastern Director of the Simon Wiesenthal Center

"A fascinating story that takes a reader inside an already wounded family toiling through horrific difficulty in the pursuit of life itself. ... It forces readers to ask themselves if they could endure a struggle or whether they might support another person in a life or death battle. This angle makes the book valuable for teachers to use and beneficial for students to read at the high school level."

— Lawrence M. Glaser
Executive Director, New Jersey Commission on Holocaust Education

"A moving and inspirational tribute to survival. The story in *"Together"* becomes our story. It is told with such vivid and poignant detail that the reader becomes part of the family. And so every reader proudly shares in the responsibility to remember and retell these inspirational stories for the sake of generations to come."

— Rabbi David S. Widzer
Temple Beth El of Northern Valley

"Together is a story that demands re-telling. It's an important addition to the voices of survivors who will live on through the telling of their tales."

— Robin Raskin
contributor, *Huffington Post*

"Arnold's perspective is colored not only by those non-Jews who saved her father's family but also by her experience visiting Brzostek as an adult."

— Johanna Ginsberg
New Jersey Jewish News

"What an inspiring story about three survivors who can teach us much about faith, courage, and sheer human strength."

— Nido R. Qubein
President, High Point University

"*Together: a Journey of Survival*, shows how brightly the human spirit can shine even in the darkest of times."

— G. J. Phoenix
bestselling author of *Seat of God*

"I was lucky enough to read an advance copy of *Together*; it is a thrilling and riveting story that you will not be able to put down."

— Hayley Dinerman
Executive Director, Triple Negative Breast Cancer Foundation

"Incredible Story"

—*Northern Valley Press*

"This story is about a mother's love and the incredible strength in that bond. Sala Schonwetter's story resonates with anyone who understands the extremes you go to for your children."

— Ricki Fairley
Thought Leader, Dove Marketing

TOGETHER
A Journey for Survival

Ann S. Arnold

 Avalerion Books, Inc.
www.avalerionbooks.com
Miami, Florida

AUTHOR'S NOTE

This book is based on the memories of my father, Mark, and my Aunt, Zosia, not to mention the stories we heard from my grandmother Sala growing up. Some names have been changed, some dates may be off. The spirit however is quite real.

To my father, Mark, my grandmother, Baba Sala, and my Aunt Zosia for inspiring me beyond what words can describe.

For my children, nephews and cousins – May our legacy live on through you and inspire you to remember that everything is possible.

.

CONTENTS

ACKNOWLEDGEMENTS

There are so many people to thank that have helped me along my own journey. Dad, you are my hero and my everything, thank you for all you have shared, and even those things you wished you never had to think of again. To my aunt Zosia, thank you for all your time and memories. Maximillion, my mentor, my book whisperer, my friend, I will never be able to thank you enough for all you have done. John, who gave patience in equal measure with his expertise. To my mother, sister, family and friends that have encouraged me every step of the way, you know who you are, thank you. And to my husband, Jonathan, and children, Ashley and Lexi, you are what gets me up every morning, thank you for your everlasting patience, support and love.

The Question: Who?
The Answer: Me
The Question: Where?
The Answer: Here
The Question: How?
The Answer: Within
The Question: When?
The Answer: Now
The Question: What?
The Answer: Never Forget

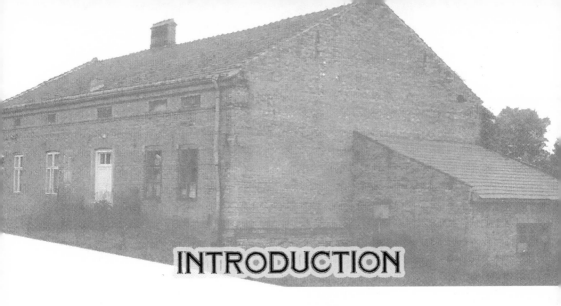

INTRODUCTION

by Ann S. Arnold

My father has always believed that he is living on borrowed time. In all honesty, it's a miracle he survived his childhood. Maybe that's why he lives life with such enthusiasm – easily embracing each new experience and collecting friends wherever he goes. How else could I explain my first day in college? Other parents helped their children move in, said their tearful goodbyes, and left for home. Not my father. I found him at a popular fraternity house, beer in hand, surrounded by brothers who were hanging on his every word. There he was, completely at ease and fully enjoying his newfound status as an honorary freshman.

Yet most people do not realize the horrors he has overcome. Telling people you are a Holocaust survivor is not a great conversation starter. My sister and I grew up hearing my father's stories. Looking back, I can see how he toned them down for us when we were little. Even as a teenager, I am not sure I truly grasped the awfulness of his experience or the immense strength it took to survive. Not until I had my own kids and began to work on my blog and this book did I realize just how astonishing my family history is.

In 1939, only fifteen hundred people lived in their village of Brzostek in southern Poland. Of those fifteen hundred people, five hundred were Jewish. Three years later, less than fifty of those five hundred villagers were still alive. The only reason my grandmother, father, and aunt were among them is because they fled their home and spent the long years of the war in an endless search for survival.

When the German army invaded Poland in 1939, my father was a six-year-old prankster living in the house of the most prosperous family in his village. Back then, the Nazis were fervent not only in their desire to murder Jews but also in their belief that Poles were generally inferior. My grandfather quickly went from prestigious farmer and landowner to working on slave crews. One day his family received word that they were to be rounded up, and my grandmother with her two children escaped with little more than the clothes on their backs.

Three long, terrible years followed. Forced to flee their home, they were herded into a four-block ghetto in the nearby town of Dembitz, where they watched fellow Jews die in the streets. Thanks to their kind Gentile neighbor from back home, they fled just before the Nazis corralled the remaining Jews and sent them in cattle cars to Auschwitz. As near skeletons they wandered through the forest, taking shelter in the winter months with sympathetic Polish families. With the S.S. troops relentless in their hunt for Jews, they had to take refuge wherever they could find it. From living under hay stacks in attics, to living in graves under pigsties, this became their new normal.

I have always thought it amazing that my father could come from such horrors as a child and yet view life so brightly. Perhaps it is exactly because of his childhood that he regards life like a precious gift.

Outside Yad Vashem, the Holocaust museum in Israel, is a long Wall of Honor bearing the names of thousands of selfless non-Jews who risked their lives to save Jews during the Holocaust. There is no greater honor than to be recognized on this incredible monument in what is known as the Garden of the Righteous. Many of those recognized are Polish, like the selfless people that took in my family. Thanks to the spirit, courage and strength of those people, my father, grandmother and aunt survived.

This is their story.

CHAPTER ONE

September 1, 1939

It was an excellent year. The spring had been wet, the summer hot. The earth had responded with gratitude by bestowing on the small village of Brzostek, Poland, a plentiful yield for all of their crops. The town square was bustling with villagers shopping for their daily necessities and food at the local outdoor market. Sala Schonwetter could almost taste the sweetness of the tomatoes, the crispness of the lettuce just by walking past each stand. As she left the butcher with her fresh meat, she added it to the bags she carried that already held the salt and sugar she had bought earlier.

She was dressed in a white shirt and royal blue skirt. Her black hair was pulled snugly behind her head in an efficient bun, and her olive features were darkened by the endless hours in the sun. As she left the square, she looked out over the lush rolling hills filled with neat, pretty little homes, their flower beds bursting with bright colors behind white picket fences lining the streets. As she passed one of the homes on her way out of town, she waved at the young woman cradling a nursing infant in the front yard. Everyone knew one another, accepting their differences as part of the warp and weave of small town life.

Just outside the center of the village, down the only paved road, Sala approached the largest farm in the area. The Schonwetter family owned numerous acres of land, but they lived unpretentiously. Israel was the head of the Jewish community in the village, as his father had been, and his father before, a line of Jewish leaders, Galicia landowners, who were known to be fair and honorable. Wealthy and successful, Israel was well respected not only by his peers, but also by all that worked for him.

To the right, just off the road, stood the family's two-story red brick house, highlighted by a row of beautiful violets. Running past the house was a dirt road that led to the farm's outbuildings and the fields beyond. The first barn, on the left, was surrounded by cattle and a team of horses. Their second barn was visible just before the line of a stone fence. It was filled with crops of rye, wheatberry, and beets from their summer efforts. To one side of the barn sat fresh hay they collected from the legumes, stored for later use in the stables. Even the bins in the basement overflowed with potatoes.

Once Sala had put away her purchases, she called out for her son. "Manek? Manek ... where are you?"

Sala walked out onto the elevated porch at the back door of their house, her deep brown eyes intently sweeping the farm. As she descended the stairs, she ran into Heniek, one of her husband's most loyal and hardworking young men.

"Have you seen Manek?"

He smiled. "Playing games again, is he?"

"Isn't he always? But there is a time and place for everything. If you see him, please let him know I am looking for him."

"Of course, ma'am."

Sala headed toward the barn, continuing her search. She passed one of the plows, resting on the side wall. The horse that had been drawing it greedily lapped up the water from the trough.

Hiding behind the stack of hay, the boy watched his mother calling and searching for him. The barn with the horses was where he liked to hide the most. The fields surrounding the house were dotted with men hard at work, harvesting the final crops before the winter cold came. He'd waited until his mother went upstairs to get his younger sister, Zosia, before running as fast as his five-year old legs would take him out the wood plank door, across the backyard, through his mother's empty vegetable plot, to dive behind the haystack.

Sala waved at her husband, Israel, and came over to the fence where he was hitching the wagon. Manek hid his laughter behind his hand. He would not be drawn from his new favorite hiding spot unless his father turned, put his hands on his hips, and called him by his full name: "Mendel Schonwetter!" This is how he knew Poppa was serious. Although he was very strict, he was kind. The only time Manek remembered him yelling was when he was very young and had tried to "help" him in the vegetable garden by digging up unripe lettuce. He thought they were weeds! Now he wanted to stay out with Poppa as he went to check on the men working in the field. Not stuck working on the garden with his Mamusia and baby sister.

"I cannot find Manek. I thought he would help me with the weeding."

"Sala, you know how much he loves to be outside with the horses. Let the boy be."

"The boy needs to learn—"

"And he will." Israel put his arms around Sala and gave her his special smile. It was the one which made his blue eyes twinkle. "Manek will learn everything you wish him to. We will teach him."

"We may have to. I have no interest in sending him to that school, where they'll insist he act like a good Polish boy."

"He is a good Polish boy. One who happens to be Jewish."

"Then he should wear his Keppalah even if they don't like it."

"Perhaps we'll get the Jewish school open again. If not, we'll teach our Manek at home. If I could help you understand math, I could teach my son whatever he needs to know."

Israel's blue eyes mischievously sparkled with the memories. She had been only sixteen at the time, and he had fallen in love instantly. Even at his age, she was worth the eight years he had to wait for her hand.

"The only reason you tutored me in math was so you could spend time with me when my father refused your suit." Sala countered, answering his knowing smile.

"He made us wait until your sisters were wed, as is fitting, as is custom. Besides, you were worth it." They shared a kiss.

Sala was the youngest of nine children. Half of her siblings had moved away to a far-off land called America during the vicious pogroms of the First World War, many years ago. She had never met her eldest sister, who had left before Sala was born. The four younger ones had remained with their parents. Her father, Mendel Beim, was a devout orthodox Jew who believed that there was a proper order to all things. He was a farmer, and she had learned the way of the land from him.

He knew of the Schonwetters, since they were the wealthiest landowners in Zabka. These were Israel's cousins. Israel's father and brother owned much of the land in all the surrounding villages, and Israel had been given the parcel in Brzostek, while his cousin inherited the one in Zabka. When Israel had first met Sala while visiting his cousin, her older sisters, Mala and Rivka had not yet wed. He fell in love quickly, saying that he only had eyes for her. According to tradition, though, the eldest females must wed prior to the younger ones. Israel was given that option, and he refused any of the sisters. He waited eight long years to finally marry Sala, yet he had no ill will toward her father. He understood and respected the man. When Sala's family lost their farm, he even took them in, housing them in the apartment attached to his house, until their deaths a few years back.

The two parents ignored the giggles coming from the corner of the paddock behind the hay. This game of Manek hiding so he could spend more time with the horses had been going on all summer, and at this point they were used to it. There was plenty of news from Tarnow of bad things coming. Better their oldest child take all the time he could to enjoy life.

"What did the Rebbe say?"

"He knows less than we do," Israel shrugged.

"What do we …"

"Sala, we do what we planned," Israel stated emphatically. "We have no choice."

"But how?"

Israel smiled again and Sala felt she could breathe a little easier at the confidence in his gaze. "We stay together, my love. This is what we do. This is what we always to do in order to survive."

She bit at her lip. "We should have gone to America—"

"There was no time to join your brother and sisters there. And besides, we love Brzostek. This is where my father, mother and grandfather are buried. This is where our friends are. This is where we'll stay together. We're far from the railroad. The Germans don't want anything to do with our little village."

"Our little village is filled with Jews." Sala's dark eyes were shiny with worry.

"We are a community, Sala. Our neighbors love us."

"They love you. They tolerate the rest of us. I can only pray love will be enough."

"Love is always enough." Israel turned to the hay bales and crossed his arms over his chest. "Now, Mendel, did you hear your Mamusia …"

A roar filled the sky. Manek came out from the hay with his head tilted all the way back as he stared into the blue expanse above them. "Poppa, what are those birds? I've never seen such birds. They are so large and noisy!"

"Planes?" Sala gasped.

"War planes," Israel stated. He drew his wife closer to his body and his eyes continued to stare at the planes and the direction they took.

Manek couldn't stop watching the sky, fascinated by the great winged beasts that just changed his idea of all that was in the world. "There are so many of them, Poppa. They blot out the sun."

Animosity between Poland and Germany stretched back centuries. However, recently, the increased talk of the rise of the man called Hitler had everyone on edge. Jews in particular were starting to feel the restlessness and danger around them. Israel's own two sisters, who had moved to Magdeburg years before, had written that conditions for Jews were deteriorating. One of his sisters had written a few years back that she and her family had decided to leave Germany for Palestine. Another sister and her husband had left Germany as recently as a year ago, coming back to Poland. They spoke of soldiers in brown shirts and Kristallnacht, a night when synagogues, homes, and Jewish-owned businesses were plundered and destroyed in a Nazi-inspired pogrom.

Manek and his parents continued to watch as one wave after another of war planes continued to roll past them. Manek stepped closer to Israel. He wished to show them how brave he was and how grown. Though he believed he was old enough to be with the men, the little boy still stayed near his Poppa so he could put his arm around him, too. He might wish to prove he is grown, but nothing was better than his father's embrace. Israel was brave, wise and kind. Sala knew Manek wished to be all those things as well.

"What do we do?"

Israel squeezed his wife's shoulder. "What we discussed. Sala, I'm not worried. We're far away from the big towns. It will take forever before the Germans even think of coming here."

"You are an optimist."

"That is not a crime. What are you?"

"A wife and mother."

The smile they shared lasted a few moments longer than usual, which surprised Manek. He was used to his parents being special with each other, but lately, their hugs lasted longer. They looked at each other as if they were afraid this was the last time. In Manek's world, there had always been Schonwetters in Brzostek. There would always be Schonwetters here.

"Come, Manek." Mamusia followed her command with a firm hand on the back of his neck as she dragged him to the house.

She gave him a small basket, pointed him to the first row of flowers, and then disappeared inside to get his sister. He was not allowed near the vegetable garden, where lettuce, cucumbers and tomatoes were grown, not after the last time when he had tried to help and only succeeded in ruining a section of the plot. Normally, he hated to be relegated to the flowers, but Manek's mind continued to teem with thoughts of the planes he'd seen. "What did it mean? What was going to happen? *And when will I get to ride on one?*"

When Sala came back out with Zosia, she also carried her good coat and sewing kit. Placing the toddler on a blanket, she settled in a chair and laid out needle and thread. Manek watched, puzzled, as Sala turned the garment inside out and started to work on it.

"Mamusia, what are you doing?"

"I need to put in some new pockets."

"Why?"

"This must happen to all of our coats," she explained. "It's to hide special things. To keep our secrets. You must never tell anyone, Manek. Promise me, please, or I will not let you spend time with the horses anymore."

This was the most dire punishment she could inflict on him. His father taught him about honor. If he gave a promise, he had to mean it. "I won't, Mamusia. I'll never tell anyone."

"You are a very good boy."

Manek smiled, and Sala swallowed hard as he became the embodiment of his father before her eyes. She hunched over her sewing so he could not see the tears. Silently she prayed, "He's a child. Please God, let him have his time to be a child."

She knew now it was not going to be a good year after all.

CHAPTER TWO

May 20, 1940

The Germans came and took all of the color from the world. Their gray uniforms seemed to suck all the vivid beauty from the countryside in which she was born. Israel still believed in the kindness and loyalty of the townspeople. Yet as the demands of the occupiers grew in intensity and frequency, she could no longer agree with her husband's positive outlook. To her, every face had a dark cast to it. She feared enemies everywhere, lurking among even her oldest acquaintances. The warnings from her mother and grandmother were always foremost in her mind. Stories of the Russians and their persecution during World War I, the brutish behavior the soldiers had freely inflicted on Jewish women. Her mind kept reviewing her family's warnings, as well as the long walks she once took with her grandfather, through the forest, far from another soul.

Israel was such a good-hearted man, he always saw the best in those around him. He trusted completely in his faith and God. Sala, on the other hand, at an early age had been taught to pay attention to everything around her, and to never trust anyone at face value. She had grown up with religion, but her mother had always told her that God does not put food on her table, hard work does. Her long walks with her grandfather were laden with subtle clues on how to survive, what to look for, and how to live off the earth. She did not even realize she was learning valuable life lessons. She only knew how happy those shared moments were for her.

The peace she felt in those days was only a refuge, however, from the horrors overtaking them now. Considering the news they were occasionally able to catch on Rebbe Wolkenfeld's radio and from the friends who worked in the army barracks, they were relatively blessed. She was not displaced from her home, and although it was not much, she was still able to provide some food for her children. The Germans treated her people as a slave labor force. Wizened scholars and trades people dragged into fields to work land they received no benefit from. Even her husband and her brother were regularly lined up to toil at paving roads and building walls. All to help the Germans, their enemy, strengthen the grip they were using to strangle her homeland.

To make matters worse, they were using the Schonwetter home as their gathering point. When they first came to town, they had spent time figuring out the lay of the land, and they ended up on her doorstep to announce that they were now in charge. They would be using the nicest house, including her beautiful gardens and yard, to determine the fate of her neighbors and loved ones. Each day they would come and separate the men into different groups. Some would be taken out on wagons to work far from home, while others worked tirelessly in their own backyard for the benefit of their enemy. Each day they would go out to work, and each night return, drained.

The effect on Israel was immense. His once jovial attitude was replaced by despair and fatigue. He used to love going into the fields, working side by side with his crews. Now he dreaded getting out of bed. He would wake each morning not knowing if he would be sent to the fields to work, or have to endure the hardships of manual labor repairing a nearby road. He would return in the evening, barely having eaten all day, drenched in sweat and wearing a look of defeat in his eyes.

To make matters even worse, if that was possible, the Germans had relocated Captain Zeidler and his wife to Brzostek to be in charge of the regional Polish police and monitor matters. The couple had taken an unusually keen interest in her Zosia. All that blonde hair, and those beautiful blue eyes she had inherited from Israel, were like a magnet to the couple. Their constant visits with chocolate and gifts for her baby girl worried Sala beyond words, but what could she do?

The only consolation she had was that her parents had passed away before Manek was born to not have to endure these terrors.

Sala stood outside on her porch, watching the men in the fields across her home. Her husband and brother were hard at work as always. They were easy to distinguish even from this distance due to the bright yellow stars they now wore on their chests. Last November the Nazis had ordered that all Jews in Poland had to wear them, and their little house, usually so filled with laughter, was strangely quiet that evening. She had stayed up all night having to sew them on their clothes. The Pilats, who rented a room in the home and were more like family than boarders, stayed far from her place by the fire. She wiped away the tears in her eyes at the memory of one of their six children asking why the Schonwetters were getting gold stars and what they did to deserve it.

Little did the young realize the badge was a way to mark them.

They were such good people, the Pilats. When she had first married Israel, and moved into his family home, she never would have imagined she would gain such a wonderful extended family. If only they could go back to the way they were, when the biggest difference between them was the number of children they had.

The winter had been long and lonely. Spring was a blessing, a chance to replenish the food that had evaporated from the larder.

Behind Israel, walking with the same lolling gait, his hands crossed behind his back as he studied the dirt beneath his feet, was her Manek. Her little boy was growing fast into a man, one with her dark coloring. They stood out from the blonde-haired Polish people as bright as the lights on the Germans' automobiles. It made her even more scared.

Watching her husband and brother run over to where one of the men was trying to move a stump from the additional field, she prayed this would be a great harvest. They'd need the food. The Wehrmacht, Germany's regular army, was a great ravenous beast, always in need of more supplies. Not only did they fail to pay for their bounty, but Israel would even give them gifts each time they came to keep them satisfied and happy. Most of what they'd harvest would go to feed their oppressors.

They were not what kept her up at night, however. Even during this nightmare they were still able to get news, and none of it was good. As scary as the soldiers were, the SS were a fresh depth of terror. Descriptions of their dark uniforms and even darker tempers filled her with fear she could not describe. They were known as brutal soldiers that spread terror wherever they went. She had heard from Israel's sister of the terrifying way they had come into her hometown just before she and he husband decided to leave for Poland.

Sala feared their true enemy was still on their way.

Suddenly, she realized she could no longer see her son basking in his father's shadow. A whinny echoed on the breeze, and she could vaguely make out Manek climbing up on the seat of the wagon. Israel yelled and started to run toward the horses, but Sala knew he would be too late.

Manek raised the reins, flicked them in the same fashion as his father, and gave a mighty roar.

The horses, overjoyed to finally be freed to do something, immediately responded. It was a young team, filled with the energy bursting from the muscles and bones of youth. Their first lunge threw Manek back and they went running. Sala's heart pounded so hard, she could feel it throughout her body.

A roar filled the air. The sound of a multitude of large engines coming down the road heralded the arrival of more Germans. A never ending wave of them.

Sala watched, helplessly, as Israel ran after the racing wagon. Her only son had stood up in the seat, yelling and laughing, as the horses started. Then Manek lost the reins with the first lunge of the wagon. He was now simply holding on for his life.

One heartbeat.

Sala swiftly recognized the row of cars coming down the road. They were filled with the black uniforms of the SS.

Another heartbeat.

She could trace the line of the team of horses cutting across the road, straight to the barn where they knew they'd be fed, watered and rubbed down. Her fists tightened, nails cutting into her palms, drawing blood.

Sure enough, just as her mind's eye drew it, the team of horses raced straight for home, nearly clipping a uniformed soldier on a motorcycle. She didn't think. She couldn't. She leapt in front of the team and wrenched the wagon to a stop. She knew what she had to do.

She snatched her child from the seat and dragged him down to the ground. She couldn't acknowledge the stunned horror on Manek's face. His open mouth, the hurt in his eyes, the evaporation of his father's smile.

"What were you thinking? How dare you touch your father's wagon?"

Behind her, she could hear the motorcycle come to a stop.

"I have told you to stay away from the horses." She pulled him up, dragging him by the elbow. "I've warned you no good comes from your tricks." She shoved him violently. "You have to learn, Manek."

A hand stilled her fist, which was clenched in despair. Looking up, she gulped at the hardness in the SS officer's gaze. She looked up at his hat, noticing the embroidered eagle that looked ready to fly off his perch and swarm in on her. "Your boy almost killed me."

"I know." She shook off the soldier's hold so she could reprimand her stunned son again. His cheeks were bathed with tears and—was that blood? Sala felt the gorge choke her. She'd never raised her hand to anyone, much less her own child. This was her baby, her precious son. His face, the betrayal in his eyes, his astonishment. She whacked his backside. Better her hand than the soldier's fist. Or God forbid, the SS officer's gun. "That's why I'm beating him. How dare he endanger your life and the horses?"

Somewhere she could sense Israel and David were witnessing her greatest shame. Pulling Manek up again, she turned him around so she could strike his backside another time.

Feeling the soldier's eyes on her, boring through the clothes on her back, she continued to strike her child.

"Okay, okay." This time when the arm covered in the black and silver of an officer stayed her actions, the eyes she looked into had softened. "Enough. Just make sure he'll never do such foolishness again."

"I will. Thank you, sir."

Sala remained frozen, her sobbing son draped over her arm. She waited, her heart sickened, her stomach a pit of acid. It took all her strength to not double over and retch right there and then. They all stayed as still as statues as the soldier got back on his motorized horse and rode after his friends. Her shame increased as she saw the horror in her husband's and brother's faces. Manek stayed on her arm, crying and shaking.

"David, take my son inside and help him clean up."

Manek was extracted from her hold by her brother, who never once met her gaze.

When she heard the door close behind them, Sala ran to the side of the house to the well. The bucket already had water in it, so she plunged her hands inside. The freezing water chilled her fingers, sending needles of ice into her bones. She kept plunging her hands into the water, rubbing them. Blood. There was blood on her hands. Her child's blood? So much blood. Oh God, what if she hurt him?

Israel tried to draw her away from her washing, but she shook off his hold. She had to get her child's blood off her hands. "Sala ..."

Shaking her head, she continued to wash her hands, trying to clear them of the red stain of her guilt. "I had to do it," she whispered. "He would have killed him. You know he would have killed him. You've heard what they do, and they're allowed. He would have killed our child."

"I know." He tried to pull her away from the bucket, but Sala would not be moved. "He was SS, Sala. He would have killed Manek and the horses, and been commended for it. I know you did the right thing." She continued to scrub. "Sala." He plunged his hands into the water with hers and forced her fingers to unclench. "It's your blood, not his. He'll be fine. Please, Sala. He will be fine."

"How?" Her entire body shook with the sob that almost jackknifed her into the well. "How will any of us be fine, again?"

Israel pulled her into his embrace, burying her face in the wool of his coat. His arms were steel bands around her. When she knew that no one would hear her cries, buried in the force of her husband's embrace, she finally released them. And then she realized. The Germans didn't just take the color from the world, they took emotion and decency and honor as well.

Now all that was left was heartbeats. How much longer could they last?

CHAPTER THREE

Manek walked tall down the road to town. He was seven years old now. A man. Mamusia had arranged for a tutor in the village square to teach him his letters, since boys with gold stars were not allowed to go to public school with other children. He didn't mind. His teacher was a nice retired lady, and the best thing was that she never said anything if he showed up late. This morning he was supposed to go over his letters with her. Poppa would be so proud when he could spell his name.

When he made it to the square, everything seemed the same as always. The stalls were open with the remaining produce of the season. The police captain was sitting outside. The Germans had taken over his station, so now he had to do most of the business in the square. People were going into the bank, children running to get into the schoolhouse before the teacher grew angry.

Everyone kept their head down and moved quickly.

Something was wrong, though. Different.

The Germans. He couldn't see any Germans.

Rather than proceed to the retired teacher's house and learn his lessons, he whirled around and rushed back toward home. He'd learned since the day he stole the wagon. Things were never going to be the same again. No laughter. No tricks. Poppa no longer spoke of prayers at the Shul. Mamusia did not smile.

Most of all, he had learned when the Germans are doing

something, you have to know what it is. You have to know where they are.

Manek had heard his parents talking in whispers during the night, when they thought the children were sleeping. He could hear the fear in their anxious voices. Rumors were swirling of violence, unexplained disappearances, and no one knew what to make of such harshness or what it meant. His own cousins had come from Germany a few months before. They had left their homes in fear, over what the Nazis were doing to their neighbors and in their small town. When they arrived, the stories they told were unbelievable. Could they all be true? He could not imagine leaving his home, so it must have been really horrible to make them flee.

When he reached his property, he paused in the tree line to watch. Crouching down, he wrapped his arms around the tree to help keep his balance. Poppa and Uncle David were standing at one side of a table that had been brought outside, their dining table if he guessed right. Two German officers were sitting at the table, and in front of them stretched a long line of people. All of them from Brzostek, all of them with the bright yellow star on their chests with the word *Juden*.

He was too far away to hear, but he could still see what they were doing.

The Germans were checking people on a list laid in front of them. Some of the villagers were sent to trucks parked on the road. The gray trucks were dust-covered and worn-looking. The back had an opening, and a tarpaulin cover was draped over it, covering the sides of the truck, held down by sturdy ropes. They were being divided into two groups. Some were sent to the trucks on the left, others to the trucks on the right. Manek could see Uncle David was getting angry. Poppa kept putting his hand on David's shoulder as if he were reminding him of something.

People seemed sad. Their heads down, faces sad as they were sent to the trucks, especially the ones sent to the trucks on the right. This was normal, though. The Germans came and took them away to go to work, and then they brought them back. This summons had happened many times before. Even Uncle David and Poppa had worked for the Germans.

The officer stood and yelled, words garbled and too harsh for Manek to decipher from where he sat.

Manek was stunned as the angry officer strode over to one of the people and punched him in the face.

Uncle David had enough. He lunged away from Poppa's hold to stop the officer, who turned on him. Uncle David never stood a chance. The German was bigger, stronger, and better fed. He punched Uncle David, and when he fell to the ground, the officer started to kick him.

Over. And over. And over again.

Manek held to the tree tighter, praying the beating would stop. He bit his lip to keep from crying, from screaming. His gaze returned to his father and stayed there. Trying to understand what Poppa would want him to do. He could see his Mamusia come out of the door behind Poppa, also frozen as the officer continued to kick Uncle David.

Finally, the brutality stopped.

When Mamusia and Poppa started toward David to help him, the officer yelled again. They knew not to come any closer. Just a few weeks ago, in front of their house, a Jewish man had tried to outrun the Germans. He was shot in the leg and fell to the ground, then beaten to a pulp. After, as the Polish neighbors tried to lend a hand, they were forced back, screamed at and told that if they approached the man, they would be shot dead instantly. No one had any choice but to watch in horror over the next two days as his life slowly slipped away. There was nothing they could do to help him. They did not dare to even try.

Uncle David was dragged to the right truck with the crying people and thrown into the back. He wasn't moving. He didn't make a sound. Poppa and Mamusia could only hold each other as Uncle David was driven away.

When the second truck was full, Poppa joined the rest of the people on the left. He gave Mamusia a single nod as they were taken away. Manek collapsed against the tree, his body shaking.

He'd learned after the wagon. Watch. Know. And most of all, don't be seen.

After they left, he used the forest and the fence to hide him on his way back to the house. The German officers had stayed behind. They went inside with Mamusia. She was all alone with them.

Manek was seven years old. He was old enough to help his Mamusia.

"What do you mean, you have no more eggs?"

The German officer was yelling at Mamusia and Mrs. Pilat. "You live on a farm. Farmers have eggs. Where are your eggs? Dirty Jewess. You must be hiding them from me. Is that what you're trying to do?"

"No, sir. I swear it. We don't have any chickens, so we don't get any eggs."

"I've never heard of such a thing. Where are your eggs?"

Manek could see the man draw back his fist. He was going to hit Mamusia like he did his Uncle David. No. He was a man now. He would have to protect her. "I can find you eggs."

The officers whirled around so fast to see Manek in the doorway, they almost fell sideways. One of them put his hand on his side arm. Mamusia and Mrs. Pilat's eyes grew huge, and Mamusia gave him a quick shake of the head. She didn't want him to be seen. He knew that. But he wasn't going to stand by and let his Mamusia be abused. "I know farms where we can find you eggs," he promised the officers. "Come with me. I know just the place."

"This is a farm. She must be hiding them."

"Enough," the other officer told the angry one. "Let's see what the kid can find."

"I promise." He waved them out of the house and away from his mother. "I know two families who might have eggs. I'll take you. We'll get your eggs from there. We can go right now."

He forced a smile on his face and kept walking backward, his eyes never leaving the officers. Follow, he begged in his mind. Get away from my Mamusia.

Outside, once they started walking, he felt better. He hurried to stay ahead of them. His legs were pumping so fast he was almost running. The Germans liked fast things. Cars. Motorcycles. Planes. Hopefully, even little boys. He wanted to get them their eggs and return to his home without them. He wanted to make sure his Mamusia and Mrs. Pilat were okay.

He wanted them to know he was as well.

When they got to the second farm, the Germans got their eggs. Once he saw them looking over their prize, he quickly disappeared into the trees and out of their sight. Don't be seen. Don't be known. But make sure you know where they are. What they're doing.

Back home, he accepted his hug from Mamusia, and the scolding that went with it, and went to sit down with Zosia while Sala worked on dinner.

Manek didn't ask about Uncle David.

He already knew that Uncle David would not be coming back.

CHAPTER FOUR

January 1942

They always seemed to come in trucks. The roar of the engines was the first assault, followed by the smoke and noxious fumes from the exhaust pipes. Once they hopped out of the trucks, the Germans had a gift for outdoing the bad tidings their machines heralded. On this winter day Sala stood in the yard next to her shriveled garden as the latest swarm of Germans drove up. Since the S.S. had driven past on that horrible day, she'd grown accustomed to their demands. Israel was the head of the Jewish community, so he was constantly being called into town to meet with them. He was often summoned to meet with the Germans. They wanted to make sure he would communicate calm and order to the rest of the Jewish population. Sometimes they accused him of some made-up slight, only to then absolve him of the wrongdoing, so as to evoke a false sense of fairness and security. Even worse was their use of Israel's house to organize the forced labor details.

Somewhere her brother was imprisoned in a labor camp.

Or he was lying in a grave.

That's what had happened to a good number of their neighbors. The rumors they heard from their German relatives had some truth in them, rumors always do. It's a terrible thing to pray your loved one was in a labor camp, for it was the best case scenario. Even Manek had learned by watching their neighbors disappear. German justice usually led to people being laid six feet under.

The Germans seemed to hate everyone. It felt like they had turned their rage on Poland, where the Jews were caught with nowhere to run. With the Germans occupying their land, their armies conquering vast stretches of Russia, they were trapped. There truly was no place to run, no way out.

When Israel came out of the barn they shared a look of understanding. Almost two and a half years of occupation had taught them to be ready for anything. She still remembered Manek's face the day he distracted the officers into going to look for eggs in other farms. Sala was just grateful he hadn't had to witness his uncle and his mother being beaten in the same morning.

That was the last time she'd sent her child to the tutor. As Israel kept saying, they would find a way to teach their son what he needed to know.

What he learned on his own was scary enough.

"You are the Schonwetter family?"

Israel rushed over and answered for her. It was better that way. She was always scared what would come out of her mouth. She did not possess the polite, easygoing nature her husband displayed to them. "We are, sir."

"Good. This is good."

"May we help you with something?"

"You have ten minutes to collect your belongings."

"Excuse me?"

Sala's hand went to her chest. Were they to go to the labor camp, too?

"You have ten minutes to collect your belongings. Just take your clothes. Nothing else."

"Sir, forgive me for asking, but where are we going?"

"That is not my business. Find a place to stay in town. You are no longer allowed to live here."

"Who else is going to?"

She shut out her husband and the officer's voices as she saw the people stepping out of the trucks. Volksdeutsche. Poles who were declared German in everything but nationality. They were the worst kind of collaborators, and all other Poles, Jew and Gentile alike, hated them.

"These people own your house now. Get out."

Sala ran inside and grabbed a bag. "Manek, pile your clothes together on your bed," she called to her son. Swiftly, as efficiently as possible, Sala tossed her clothing into the bag they kept under the bed, the one Israel had used once to go to Germany to visit his sister, long before they were married. Now she filled the bag with undergarments, stockings, dresses, and her favorite wool blanket, anything that she could think of that would keep them warm during the cold winter. She kept her special coat ready at all times, the secret pockets filled. She'd wear that. The items she was packing was what they'd need to survive.

When she had it filled, she grabbed the remaining case, the one she had used the day she married Israel, and rushed into Zosia's room. Such happy memories these bags represented, they hardly seemed big enough to fit so much despair. In Zosia's room she took a deep breath. She had to be smart. Little girls need so many things. She pushed her emotions away as she crammed as many clothes and outfits inside that she could fit. She looked at the special dress she had made for Zosia's last birthday. She had taken such care in sewing each stitch, so excited to see her twirl around in it when she finally put it on. The dress was getting a bit small on the ever growing child. No matter, she was taking it anyway. Nothing a needle and thread could not alter. She did not want to leave anything of any value behind for those filthy animals.

When she joined Manek, her heart stumbled at the small pile of things he had assembled.

No toys. No books. No mementos of any kind.

Her son already had an education. He hadn't learned merely reading, writing and mathematics.

He had learned how to survive.

When she went outside, Israel had run out of arguments for the German officer. The house was theirs. Poland was theirs. The Schonwetters were just inconvenient Jews, standing in the way.

"I'm ready," she announced to her husband.

"You took only your clothes?"

"Of course, sir." She looked boldly into the face of the German officer. Let him see she was not broken. She was not cowed.

As the Volksdeutsche started to file into the house, she suddenly remembered. "Excuse me, sir?" When the German looked at her, Sala consoled herself with the thought his gaze showed some small trace of respect. "The Pilat family are not Jewish. This is their house, as much as it is my husband's. Will they please be allowed to stay?"

"Now that they're not in proximity of you dirty Jews, I'm sure that'll be acceptable."

Our hands are far cleaner than yours. "Thank you. Thank you very much."

In the window, she saw Antony Pilat. He gave her a quick nod. He'd take care of things. He'd remember. He had to; she would make sure of it.

At least a friend would still be living here. "Come, Israel."

She handed her husband the two bags and led her family away. The Schonwetters had lived in this house for three generations. She had not. She knew she could survive. Looking at her cowed and shocked husband, she tried to cheer him. "Antony will still be there. He'll make sure the animals are taken care of. He'll keep watch over things," she promised Israel.

"It's my home—"

"No," she stopped her husband. "We are our home. That was just a building."

Looking down, she saw Manek gazing up at her with the same admiration and respect that he usually showed only for his father. His bag, far too big for a child his size, was almost too much for him to handle. She considered taking it from him. Helping him like the little boy he still was in that moment. But she remembered the eggs, and knew that taking the bag would insult him. She instead gave a single nod of encouragement, and Manek started to walk again. She took Zosia's small, fragile hand, and together, they all began the long trek into town. Israel kept stumbling as he continued to look behind him, but Sala noticed that her son never turned back.

Both of them kept their eyes focused straight ahead every step of the way.

CHAPTER FIVE

April 11, 1942

Tap, tap, tap. Tap, tap, tap. Sala checked on the kids sleeping nearby before she went to the window. Manek immediately sat up in bed, placing a hand on his sister's shoulder. Her son had developed a wise old man's knowledge of when he needed to be ready.

Sala sidled up to the window from one side, edging the curtain over. This wasn't their house. They had merely lived here for three months since the Nazis kicked them off the farm. That dark day an older couple who had once owed Israel money was willing to take them in. Israel had never recovered from the loss of his childhood home and farm. Although he retreated into himself, he never lost faith in God and truly believed that He would still save them. Sala was not so sure that God was listening, but she was grateful these people had given them their children's empty room, and they seemed to enjoy having the Schonwetter little ones around.

When she peered through the window, she was shocked. On the other side of the glass was Captain Ziedler's wife. Draped in a dark cloak, she had fear in her eyes. As she glanced around in the night, she gestured to Sala to come outside. Ever since the Captain and his wife had come by the other day with an abundance of chocolate for her daughter, Sala had been on alert. As they played with her sweet, innocent young girl, they had the gall to ask the child who she preferred, them or her own Mamusia. She did not blame Zosia for her answer. Chocolate was a powerful weapon to use with a hungry, small child.

Sala prepared herself to hear the worst. Israel had been taken earlier to speak with Captain Ziedler and the SS commander. They hadn't thought much about the summons at the time because it had become commonplace. Israel was still their ambassador to the local community, both Jew and Gentile alike.

Sala opened the window a bit and nodded at the other woman. Grabbing her shawl, she wrapped it around herself as she slid on her shoes. Manek moved to the other side of his sister, his eyes bright and wary. He positioned himself next to the open window. Whatever trouble she faced, she knew her son would stand beside her.

Captain Ziedler's wife hovered in the shadow of the house. Sala was almost pleased that whatever bad news she was about to be handed, her son would hear at the same time.

"You will all be taken tomorrow," the Captain's wife whispered.

"What do you mean?" Sala gasped.

"They will be here soon to gather you all up and take you away." *Where would they be taking us,* she thought? "Let me help. You know I only have a son. To have a daughter would be the answer to a prayer I have not dared breathe out loud. Zosia looks like us, she knows us and loves us. She will blend in. We will raise her as our own, at least she will survive and lead a long prosperous life."

Thunderstruck was not a powerful enough word for how Sala felt. Moments passed that felt like years, even centuries. They wanted to take her child away. At last her mind started to clear. Sala knew what she had to do. She nodded at the German woman. "Give me a little time. Let me pack a bag for her and say goodbye."

Mrs. Zeidler reached out her hand in gratitude, and Sala recoiled. "You are doing the right thing, I will be back in an hour."

Then, as quickly as she came, she vanished into the dead of night. That must be how vampires disappear.

When she pulled away from the window, she saw Manek was already getting dressed. He'd heard. He knew so much, her little boy.

She had no idea where they would be taking all the Jews. For months she had seen the trucks that had left, and some never came back. She had heard that those people were going to a work camp. Is that where they would be taking them all? Or could it be true, the rumors she heard about what happened in the larger towns and cities nearby. Where Jews had been forced to leave their homes and relocate to a small, overcrowded part of a city. What she did not know was that there were fates worse than the ones she was imagining. One thing was for sure, however, if it was dire enough for that woman to risk coming to her, it must be bad.

Sala dressed Zosia as she continued sleeping on the bed. There was no reason to rouse the child from her dreams to face this living nightmare. Besides, Zosia would fuss. She was so little, and she would not understand being taken from her warm bed and fleeing into the chill of the night. Sala perched Zosia on her hip and Manek helped her tie her shawl around her to secure the child, keeping her warm, with the illusion of safety that only a child can feel at her mother's bosom. He took her other hand as they tiptoed out of the house.

They ran on silent feet through the nearby trees. It felt as if she ran with the weight of the world on her shoulders. She did not know where to go, what to do, but knew she had to find help. Sala was grateful the fields still had the sere stalks of corn. They provided excellent cover. She made sure no one caught sight of them as she made her familiar way to her home.

Where had they taken Israel? she frantically wondered. After the house had been taken from them, his summons had become fewer and further between. He was still called occasionally into town, to council on small issues, but largely, the Germans had left him alone. The shell of a man he had become crushed her heart. His optimism and good nature had been destroyed, replaced with despair and hopelessness. He desperately wanted to find a purpose in what was happening, an explanation, but none was coming.

She knew of only one person and family she could trust completely. Her hand had barely knocked on the door before it was wrenched open. "Antony." He opened it wider to let them in, but she saw he made sure to check outside that they were not seen.

"What's happened?"

"They took him. They took Israel, and now Captain Ziedler's wife tells me they're coming for us. I don't know what to do. I don't know where to go."

He came more awake as his gaze slid over Zosia and down to Manek. "Go lie down with my children," he directed the boy. They watched Manek go to the door and pause, looking back at them. "It will be okay, Manek. Go to sleep with my children."

"We have to run—"

"They'll find you."

"Then we have to hide."

Antony shook his head. "They'll still find you. We have to hide you where they won't look."

"Where? They have everything now—"

"Sala," he cut her off. "I'll take you to my cousin's on the bicycle. In the morning he'll get you into the ghetto the Germans made in Dembitz."

"Why there?"

"You can hide with the Jews they are gathering. You'll be protected in the greater numbers there."

"I can't put you in danger—"

"We are all in danger as long as the Germans occupy our country. They'll be looking for a woman with two children, not a man, his wife and a child."

"I can't leave Manek. We have to stay together. I promised Israel and David, no matter what, we have to stay together."

"You'll be together. I'll bring Manek to you later. We must go."

Sala looked back to see her little boy still standing in the doorway, Antony's wife, Bronislawa, was next to him with a hand on his shoulder. Manek gave her a quick nod before he closed the door between them. She imagined him crawling into the bed where the six Pilat children tended to all sleep together, like a little pile of puppies. He would fall into place with all the other boys and girls. Kazimierz, Bronisz, Augustyn, Krystyna, Maria and even the eldest, Irena, they were like family. Antony would protect him. He would watch over her child. The Pilats were as close as family could be.

Outside, Antony brought around his bicycle. He helped her sit on the back with her legs hanging to the side. One arm wrapped around his waist, and the other tightly held her daughter. Miraculously, Zosia slept still, her little puffs of breath warming the crook of her neck and granting her some comfort from the despair threatening to crush her. As Antony pushed off to get the wheels turning, the night air began to rush past her face. She hoped it would keep the tears threatening to fall from coming.

In a fit of despair, she turned her head back to view the shadows she knew housed Brzostek. She had dreamt of becoming part of this place all through the years of Israel's courtship. She had loved the people here.

It was her belief when she married Israel, she'd live her entire life in this place.

Their parents died here.

She had been sure she would as well.

Now she wondered if she'd ever see it again.

CHAPTER SIX

Antony barely got back before the trucks pulled in front of the house. Manek saw the Pilats' father return when he checked on the sleeping children, his face illuminated in the waning light of the fireplace, deeply etched with exhaustion. He guessed things had gone as planned, since he didn't say anything. Manek lay back down when he saw the father go into the back of the house where he slept with his wife. The other children were lying around him in no specific order, just a pile of arms and legs, and sleeping heads. He felt Augustyn's leg in his back. The older teen was always so nice to him, not getting annoyed when a young boy just wanted to follow him around. It was warm. He could say that much for it at least. Still, he missed the comfort of sleeping next to his little sister. She never stole the covers or even hogged the bed. He slowly fell back to sleep.

He was startled awake by the banging on the door. Manek knew the Germans had come.

Don't be seen. If you are seen, make sure you're helpful. He knew the rules.

Closing his eyes, he pretended to sleep with the others. The continued knocking on the door sounded like thunder. The Germans truly did not know how to do anything in half measure.

"Where are the Schonwetters?"

Manek flinched as he remained buried in the others. "I have no idea, mein herr. I have not seen the Schonwetters since you had them evicted."

"We are looking for them."

The other children were waking up. Manek rose to his feet, his heart beating so loud he thought the sound would give him away. He kept himself close to the wall so that should the German soldiers look inside, all they would see was a group of children dressing for the day. Among six others staying hidden was easy. Antony's oldest daughter, Irena, gave him a hat, which he quickly drew on to cover his dark curly hair. Gentiles were blonde. Everyone knew that.

"Children." Antony appeared in the doorway, gazing directly at Manek first, and then, Irena. "Go do your chores now." He turned back to the Nazis and gestured to them. "Surely you don't mind if the children go outside and do their chores? There is always so much work to be done, and it is my job to tend to the roads so your trucks can travel easier."

"Yes, yes, fine."

As the children started to file out the door, Manek blended in near the end. Antony's oldest daughter lingered, to be last. When they reached the front door, one of the soldiers grabbed her by the sleeve of her dress and shook her. "How many siblings do you have, girl?"

Irena looked into the man's eyes, bold as a German, and answered without hesitation. "Seven of us, sir."

Manek hid his relief by shuffling his feet. She had included him in their number. "Seven," such a simple number, but right now it held so much power. Her quick thinking saved not only Manek's life, but the entire Pilat family. The officer counted all the children.

"Fine," the German officer shoved her into Manek. "Go."

"Allow me to give them some instructions, sir. It won't take but a minute."

Stepping outside, he ushered them all toward the barn. "You know what to do," he told his children. Turning to Manek, he drew him close so he could whisper into the boy's ear, in case the Germans were listening. Manek and he both glanced at the house and saw the officer still standing near the window. The open window. "Go into the far field, past the corn. Hide behind the old fence, Manek. You stay there, stay quiet until I come to get you. Remember, this will save yours, your Mamusia's and Zosia's life."

Manek ran as fast as he could. When he got to the fence, he tried to dig a hole behind it. Wanting to hide, to not be seen. Soon he was sure he was as far down as he could go. His body was masked by the corn plants and the stone fence.

As the long hours passed, his thoughts drifted into the past. He remembered such cheerful scenes as Uncle David walking around the house, doing his funny dance to make him laugh at the high holidays. Poppa coming in from shul, smelling like pipe smoke and prayer. He wrapped his arms around his knees and rested his forehead against them.

Wait. Be still. Be silent. Save everyone's lives. Don't be seen.

One heartbeat.

He closed his eyes.

Two heartbeats.

He bit his lips and took a breath in. Be still. Be quiet. Don't be seen. Save their lives.

Hours later, Antony came to get him. The sun had already started to set. "Manek," he said, helping him rise from the ground. Manek's legs wouldn't work, and the older man had to steady him against the stone until they remembered what their job was. It was colder than he realized. "Manek, they're gone. Let's go, boy. Let's go and find your Mamusia and your baby sister."

At any other time Manek would have been thrilled to ride on Mr. Pilat's bicycle. The trip to Dembitz flew quickly. Few people ventured out on the road in these times, other than the Germans. Fortunately, they passed none of them either. When they rolled into the small city, they saw darkened factories on their way, and Manek kept peeking at the large houses around them. This was nothing like his small village. The houses here loomed over the streets, like trees, and he could not see anything growing. Everything was just so massive. He was afraid of what he could not see almost as much as what he was. Fearful of being noticed, he forced himself to look down at the paved streets that flowed beneath the turning wheels, avoiding the witnessing eyes he imagined in the shadows.

When they got to the poorest area of the town, Manek saw they were actually riding next to a tall fence. It seemed like it went straight to the sky.

Antony pulled into an alley near the gateway. "Manek, hide." He immediately hopped off the bike and sat behind some trash cans. "I'll be back." Manek pulled his knees up again and closed his eyes. One heartbeat. Two heartbeats.

His reverie was interrupted by Mr. Pilat's voice. "Manek ... quick."

He jumped to his feet and moved to Mr. Pilat's side. "See those men?" He was indicating a group of gaunt men, wearing clothing so worn it appeared to be held together by prayer, walking slowly along the fence with their heads down. Each of them carried a piece of paper in their hands. "Go with them, like you did with my children. Use them to get you inside, boy."

"That's where Mamusia and Zosia are?"

"If all went well with my cousin, yes."

Manek hurried over to the men and sidled into their midst. He made a quick count: twenty. That should work. The guards only gave a cursory glance at the railroad workers returning from a hard day in the machine shop. It didn't matter that he lacked a work permit like the others. Getting into the ghetto was so much easier to than getting out.

Manek looked around when he was inside. He knew this place. Poppa called it Targowa Street when they used to visit. The Germans had changed how it looked, though. They had surrounded the area with tall fencing, with funny wires looped at the top with spikes coming out at all angles. A fancy building rose at the end of the long, single lane opposite the guard gate.

Then he saw her. Mamusia. He ran to her and skidded to a stop. Don't make a scene. Don't be seen. She gave him a smile, knelt and pulled him in for a tight hug. Together. They were together. Everything would be fine.

CHAPTER SEVEN

Something was wrong with Mamusia. The blank look in her eyes had started a couple of weeks ago. She had gotten so sick, it scared him. Manek overheard some other people tell Mamusia that she needed to stay away from him and Zosia. He was not sure what scared him more. The fact that she may actually listen to them or her answer: "We live together, we die together."

She had started to take food and put it into her own mouth first. She would then feed him and Zosia food out of her mouth, and almost seemed frustrated when they would wake the next morning, still healthy. She had one goal, to make them sick. She wanted to make sure that if she died, her children would die with her. They would stay together no matter what.

She finally found an old friend, one of the Kapos, the Jewish guards. She begged him to help her. To make the pain go away. He would give her something to drink every day. It was a small glass, and it smelled like the vodka Poppa used to have during holiday celebrations. After a week or so, she seemed to be feeling better, but now all she was doing was just sitting. Each day they went to get their rations, but after, she would just sit and stare into space. She was like so many of the other adults here. Lost inside their minds, overwhelmed by their grief and fear. This was not the Mamusia he knew. He needed her to get up. He needed her to give them one of her special hugs. He needed her to smile, or at least look at them fully and acknowledge what they were doing.

Manek didn't know you could be both together with someone and yet so far away.

Their home was nothing more than a small square area in the attic that they had to use an old rickety ladder to reach. They had found this space during the first few days in the ghetto. What a horrible time that was. There were just so many people here. People's homes were turned into factories, and the Germans had built barracks to house the never ending numbers of Jews entering the ghetto.

The ghetto area was small, covering a few blocks at most. People lined the dirty streets. While some tried to maintain a semblance of order, it was difficult to keep the stench of death away. There was so little food, and the conditions were so deplorable, that people would sit listlessly all along the street, and occasionally he would find himself walking over a corpse rather than a living being. Those that were put to "work" here had the unpleasant job of hauling the corpses away from the streets and from inside the homes, to some designated area the Germans had made.

The living quarters and conditions were horrible, but the ration line was terrifying. The adults who stood on it all seemed so angry and frustrated. The hollow faces stared straight ahead. No hope or joy shone in their eyes, just desperation and misery. He'd have to wait for hours on the long line, and when he got to the front, he'd be handed a small bowl of soup, if it could even be called soup—it was more like soup water—and a portion of bread. This wasn't enough food to fill him up. Even little Zosia couldn't get filled on this food. When they first got there, Mamusia would hand him her soup, and if they got bread she gave it to Zosia. It was a joke that they even called this food.

But the German officers were clear. It was all they deserved.

Now, sitting back in the attic they now called home, next to Mamusia, he tried to get her to take his bowl of soup. Mamusia had to eat. People needed to eat to survive. He knew this. She just looked at him with blank eyes. This was how Poppa acted after they were kicked out of their house. He remembered that Mamusia had said it would take him time to recover from the loss of his home. They'd have to be patient.

He didn't want to be patient now. He wanted his Mamusia back.

Zosia fretted when he handed her the bowl. She didn't like it either, but there was nothing else to eat. To make matters worse, if they could even be any worse, the Germans kept bringing more people into this place they called a ghetto. They didn't care there was no room. In the attic where they lived, they shared their space with so many people. At night, it was hard to move around all the bodies to go outside to the bathroom. Everywhere he stepped, he stumbled on more bodies of sleeping people, and some mornings he realized that the stiff ones would never wake up.

When his sister pushed away the food again he took a deep breath, hoping for patience. He had to take care of her now, take care of everything. "You must eat, Zosia," he explained. "There is nothing else, I'm sorry."

She started to get up to run. Scream out her frustration as little kids should. Manek understood her desire, but no one here wanted to hear her. They all lived with their own frustrations, and did not need to hear anyone else's. With the way Mamusia was acting, he did not want to draw any unneeded attention to any of them.. He kept thinking about the rules he'd learned. Don't be seen. Don't be heard. Pay attention to everything. Stay alive.

"Zosia," he dragged her back to Mamusia's side. "Let's do our numbers again. One ..."

She blinked at him like an owl as her lower lip started to push out, which usually heralded a crying fit. She was hungry. She was dirty. There were bugs everywhere. Their heads hurt so much from all the scratching and itching. Manek didn't blame her. He wanted to scream, too. "Two, sister. You are supposed to say two."

She still wasn't responding.

"We'll try it again. One ..."

"Mamusia," Zosia cried, pulling on Sala's arm.

She did not respond.

Manek got up and paced. He saw Mamusia's shawl lying on the floor, so he picked it up, folded it, and placed it on her lap. Walking back and forth, he tried to remember what Mamusia did when Poppa disappeared inside his mind. Together. Mamusia kept reminding Poppa they were together. Maybe Mamusia needed to be reminded.

Going to her, he dragged Zosia to kneel beside him. He took Mamusia's hands and placed them against each of their chests. "Together, Mamusia. Remember? We are together. Just like you promised Poppa."

No response.

He pushed her hands harder into their chests, until Zosia scowled. "Mamusia ... feel them. Feel us. One heartbeat." He waited a moment. "Two heartbeat." Sala blinked as if she were coming out of a trance. "What comes next, Mamusia?"

Again … silence.

Manek scratched his head and scowled at the sickening feeling of the insects walking over his fingers. Yet maybe that would be the way to get through to her. "Mamusia, I need you. There are bugs. Everywhere. I'm scared they are getting in Zosia's hair too." His sister's pale blonde hair, like sunlight, was a source of great pride for his parents. "Everyone here is sick. I don't know how to keep us well. I need your help. Zosia needs you. Mamusia … please." The second word came out as a whisper to avoid the whine he knew was building. "Mamusia, I need you."

Her eyes just stared at them, as blank as the people who lined the walls.

"One heartbeat." He pushed his Mamusia's hands to their chests. For once, Zosia was sitting quietly, not fidgeting, but instead staring so intently at her Mamusia. She missed her as much as he did. "Two heartbeats," he prompted her.

"What comes next, Mamusia?" Zosia suddenly asked.

Zosia's question finally penetrated her torpor. Sala's gaze moved over their faces, and Manek saw her actually see them. She took in their desperate, hopeful expressions. She lingered on his long hair, seeming to see the lice moving through his dark locks. Over the haggard cast of Zosia's face, the sallowness of her skin, back to the hollowed look of his cheeks. Weeks of barely eating were already taking their toll.

"Three … three heartbeats."

Manek and Zosia threw themselves into Sala's arms to hug her, overjoyed she had returned to them. She cupped Zosia's face first. When she turned to Manek, she did the same, and then smiled sadly at him. "We are going to have to shave your head."

This was when he knew they were together again, and things would be fine.

CHAPTER EIGHT

July 5, 1942

Something was wrong. Something was horribly wrong. Her friend, the baker, was busy behind the counter, people were waiting for their turn. She shouldn't feel a sense of impending doom, but she did. Sala hovered at the end of the line, trying to figure out why every muscle in her body was screaming she should run. Then she saw that she wasn't the only one feeling uneasy. Her friend's eyes were darting back and forth. To what she was doing, then Sala, and then … behind her. Someone was behind her.

That was what was wrong.

"I will have to come back," she sang out. "You are too busy now."

She hesitated outside the shop, trying to decide what to do. Once Manek had brought her out of the haze she had sunk into when they escaped Brzostek, she quickly realized they needed an additional source of food. Fortunately, she remembered a woman who ran a bakery in Dembitz. They were friends once, and the lady was kind enough to provide what extra rations she could to keep Sala and the children alive. A loaf of bread every few days was at least keeping Manek and Zosia from starving before her eyes. All she had to do was sneak out through the hole she had found in the fence and make her way to the bakery. The small opening at the bottom of the barrier was barely large enough for her to squeeze through. Not an easy feat—quite risky, in fact—but what choice did she have?

When the door opened and closed behind her, she caught the gleam of the uniform brass on the SS officers behind her.

No. Please, God, no. Life in a ghetto was a hell she had never imagined could exist. The German police, called the Schupo, was run by a man named Urban, who had no compunction about dragging Jews to the nearby cemetery and shooting them in the head, for entertainment. Gabler, the local head of the SS, was less terrifying. It was ironic to her that her own countryman was more frightening than the invader.

There was the Schupo to be frightened of, the SS to avoid if at all possible, and of course, the Kapo, the Jewish police, who were brutal in enforcing everyone else's rules. These were the known terrors she faced with each breath she took. What was worse was the fate of the unknown ones. The people in the camp talked about life beyond the fence. Some letters came in. Townsfolk would smuggle food and trade it for fine linens or jewelry, and in the process the Polish people would talk about life outside. Information, the rarest of commodities now, was available if you listened hard enough.

And that information all said the same thing. Jews were being taken away and they were never heard from again. On top of the random killings, the massacres for no reason, the Germans were making thousands of people disappear. Sala was determined she and her children would not become part of that effort.

She started to walk away from the bakery.

The Nazis did not follow.

All she could think about now was getting back to her children. Sala quickened her pace, trying to look busy. She tried to imagine how a townsperson would look right now. A busy mother who was rushing home to her non-Jewish husband and children.

Night was starting to descend, and she quickly returned to her hole and slipped back inside the ghetto. As she rushed to return home, she quickly realized she was not alone.

"Not again," she thought. Could nothing go easy for her? First the officer in the bakery, and now this.

There was no way she would lead whoever was following her back to her children, so she began to wander aimlessly through the ghetto streets. The ghetto was not large, a part of the city that was once called "Potter's Circle." It was considered one of the worst areas of town, and she never would have come here alone, at night. But now she called this home, yet walked around the four blocks feeling more fear than she could have ever imagined. Finally, one of the two German guards following her placed a hand on her shoulder to stop her and whirl her around.

"Where are you coming from?"

"Nowhere," she replied as she tightened her coat around her.

"So where are you going?"

"I am just walking . . ." she answered hesitantly, and then an idea popped in her head. "You see, I am wandering around the streets because I am so confused. I am just so hungry and tired, I don't know which way to go."

They weren't buying it. "You are lying," the taller officer stated. "We saw you crawl through that hole. Where did you go and what did you get?"

She was caught. How would she get back home? She should never have left the children. Together: she promised Israel they would stay together. Sneaking out had seemed like the only answer to her problem.

You can't stay together if your children starve to death.

Deciding honesty might be the only solution, she began to explain. "You're right. I have two children. So precious to me, my children. I would do anything for them. You understand, though, yes? You must have mamas of your own. Or maybe even wives and children. You understand about needing to do anything for your children."

They glanced at each other. At least they did not take out their guns.

She continued on, afraid if she stopped the worst would happen. "They were so just so hungry. I went out to find some bread. Something that perhaps someone had thrown away or discarded. I found a little bakery, and there was old bread in the back in the garbage. I took some for my children."

"Enough, lady," the older one held up his hands.

"Please," she swallowed with difficulty. "My children ..."

"We will let you go, but remember that if we ever see you go out again, we will kill you without hesitation. Now, get back to your children."

She did not need to be told twice.

The two men also turned to leave, and almost as if they did not care, one muttered to the other: "What difference does it make anyway? In a few days this entire ghetto will be eliminated, and they will all be dead anyway." They laughed as they walked away.

Sala kept walking with her head held high until she was sure the guards were out of sight. She hurried back to the place she now called home, and she collapsed against the brick wall outside. *What should she do? What was she going to do?*

Manek and Zosia came out from the house. Her son was holding his sister's hand, but they immediately froze as they sensed something was wrong.

Sala straightened. She'd find a way. They always found a way. Nodding to them, she ushered them back inside to go to sleep. They'd have to find a way in the morning. She only hoped it would not be too late.

CHAPTER NINE

The next day, Sala felt a familiar frustration. Half the day disappeared just getting the rations. She'd gone too long not thinking. Just surviving. She remembered her grandfather's lessons in the forest, and she was determined to never make that mistake again. Standing on the line for food, she started to go through their options to escape.

Where should she go? Who would come with them? How would they get to whatever place they decided to go? There were no answers, just an endless stream of questions filing through her brain.

All she was sure about was they had to go tonight.

She was equally sure that before she took her son and daughter on the run, she needed a plan. Hopefully, she would be able to find someone who was willing to help them. Sala couldn't imagine managing the escape without some help.

But who?

Looking at the people in line around her, those sitting on the ground, loudly slurping down the watered gruel the Germans called soup, she started to mentally rule each one out. Not the old. No other families. One little girl who loved to laugh loudly would be more than enough to handle.

Who?

Who should she tell? Who would come with her?

She couldn't tell everyone. Mass panic would only make the Germans move faster, or worse, they'd send in Urban and his goons.

Then she saw Isaac. Her cousin.

Following him, she was shocked to discover not only had he been in the ghetto for a while, so were two of her other cousins, Bunek and Ringel.

"Sala?" Isaac hugged her tightly. She embraced each of these familiar forms, grateful to find a friendly face at last, and she just found three. Perhaps this was the answer she needed.

"How is Israel?"

Sala shook her head at Ringel's question, not able to put into words her fear over her husband's fate or her concern he could not have survived. He would have found them by now if he had. "I'm here with only Manek and Zosia."

The three men looked away, instantly uncomfortable. She sensed that they were feeling guilty about something, and she realized what it was.

"You know."

"Know what?" Bunek scuffed at the dirt with his shoe.

"About the liquidation. They're going to kill all of us. We have to do something."

"We're going to do something, all right. What will you do?"

Sala shook her head at Ringel's question. "I don't understand you question, what will you do? I have to take the kids and escape. You can help me. Please. If you have a plan already, take us with you." By this point she could see that they did have a plan. "Please. I need help—"

"Are you crazy? There's no way we can take two little kids, if we even find a way out."

Isaac held his hand up to stop Ringel. "Wait, maybe we can—"

"No. It's been decided." Bunek folded his arms over his chest.

Sala could feel the opportunity slipping away from her. She didn't mind pleading with them for her children's sake. "You know me. You have eaten at my father's table, my husband's table. Israel has helped each of you. Now I'm asking, begging you if I must, to help me. Help my children. Please. I know things, I might be just who you need—"

"No. You cannot come, not with two small children."

Sala felt her anger rising. Her mouth fell open at the finality in Ringel's voice. She wanted to yell. To be just like Zosia and let all of her frustration show. Yet a show of rage wouldn't help. It certainly wouldn't persuade them to do what she needed the most. She left them without another word, never looking back.

She had fallen into a feverish reverie as she blindly wandered the blocks, when a tug pulled her away from her dark thoughts. "Excuse me. You are a Schonwetter, right?"

Looking down into a small boy's face, she nodded.

"A man over on the other side of the barbed wire, by that house, told me to go find the Schonwetters and bring them back there. He wanted to talk to them. You are her, right?"

"Yes. Show me."

When she rounded the corner of the building, Sala almost fell to her knees when she saw Antony standing at the fence. He looked the same as always, though the dark bags under his eyes were new. "Antony Pilat," she said, staggering into the fence. As their hands met through the links, she felt stronger already.

"Sala, I do not have good news."

"The ghetto?"

"Heniek works as a guard at the jail. He overheard them talking and told me. Tomorrow the entire ghetto … the Germans are going to kill everyone without a work permit. You and the children are in danger."

She swallowed so hard, she heard it. "I don't know what to do."

"I have a plan. Get the children and meet me back here tonight. I will get you all to safety."

"Antony, I—"

Her gratitude for his generosity choked her harder than any noose could. Antony smiled, shook his head and squeezed her hands again. "Sala, get the children ready and meet me back here tonight."

CHAPTER TEN

July 6, 1942

She waited for the darkest hour. Luckily, there were plenty of clouds to cover the light of the moon. Returning to the spot where she had seen Antony in the afternoon, she was sure for a moment he had failed her. He'd changed his mind or been caught by the SS. She couldn't use the hole in the barbed wire fence she'd been using to get extra food. The Germans had not only closed it, they also put a guard in front of it.

Then Antony Pilat stepped out from the shadows of the doorway holding a blanket. "I'm here," he said, smiling. He managed to throw the blanket over the razor wire on the top of the fence with one heave.

"The children will never be able to climb so high." she remarked as she pulled her son and daughter closer to the fence. As she did, she realized Antony would see just how thin they'd all grown.

"Your Mamusia shaved your head?"

The question was enough to make Manek smile, and even Zosia, out of sorts since being woken up earlier for a surprise walk, joined in. "She took me to a man with clippers," Manek answered.

"Better that than her kitchen knife, no?"

"Antony …"

"You have to get them over, Sala." He indicated the fence, her arms and the children. "I'll catch them. I swear it."

Sala drew in a deep breath as her eyes swam with tears. The terror of her children being hurt beat at her like a physical beast, but she recognized they had no other choice.

She had to do it. She just didn't know how.

If she had still talked to God perhaps she would have asked him for help. Instead, deep in her heart, she called to her husband. *Israel, I need your strength. Give me your arms, just this once.*

Help me do this.

As she gazed at the children, Manek pushed Zosia closer to her. He wanted his little sister to go first. If she saw Mamusia throw him over first, she might get so scared she would start crying, or even worse, refuse to take her turn and start to cause a scene. He innately knew they could not take that chance. Picking up her daughter, she cuddled her close to her chest. "Coreczka, you know how much Mamusia loves you, yes?" Her eyes wide, Zosia solemnly nodded her head. She kissed her child's cheek. "Your Mamusia loves you so much because you are pretty and kind, and you are—"

Without finishing the sentence, Sala hurled her child up into the air, closing her eyes. Her arms burned, and her shoulders felt as if they had been wrenched out of the sockets, but she had to throw her over that razor-covered wire.

Israel, she called in her heart, let her be brave.

When she didn't hear a cry, she opened them to see Zosia safely nestled in Antony's arms ... on the other side of the fence.

As she turned to Manek, he stepped closer to her. Without need for direction, he folded his arms over his chest and nodded. "You can do it, Mamusia. Don't worry. Mr. Pilat will catch me."

This time she managed to keep her eyes open when she threw her child over the fence. Antony caught him easily in his arms. "You next, Sala."

"Who will throw me?"

He smiled. Perhaps, if they could still find a way to see humor in the situations they faced, the Germans would not succeed in taking all the color from their world. "Climb to the top of the fence and then jump. I will catch you, too."

"I'll help him, Mamusia."

She felt as if she could fly at this point. The wire fence was easy to climb, though decades had passed since her time of running after her brothers into the forest and climbing trees. At the top she had to go slower. Even though the blanket was covering most of the curl of the razor sharp wire, it was tricky to maneuver over it. Finally, she managed to climb over the wire and get to the other side without being cut. "Jump," Antony ordered her from the ground. When she did, she made sure to keep hold of the blanket, determined to leave no trail behind of what they'd done.

His arms closed around her and set her down on her feet. Manek gave her a hug, though Zosia's look of hurt outrage for being thrown over a fence cut her straight to the heart. "Quickly," he said, pointing at a little house in the nearby lane, where he'd come from with the blanket.

Inside the house, Sala was startled when she saw a man passed out in front of the fire. "Don't worry about him." Antony shut the door behind them. "I poured enough vodka down his throat to drown the entire German army. He will be sleeping for hours, I am sure."

"What of his family?"

"Sleeping off the kielbasa and vodka I fed them earlier. It took longer for this one to pass out."

"Antony," Sala said, looking at all the bottles on the table. "How can I ever repay you?"

"You are my family." He picked up a pile of fabric from the bench. "These people paid me back with new clothes for you. I know what the conditions are like in the ghetto. Change into these and we will go. I found a family to take you in, and they'll keep you safe straight through the winter."

She gave Zosia clothes and helped her pull off her soiled, grimy dress. "New clothes, my daughter. Won't that be nice?" The little girl began to pull on her fresh garments. Looking up, Sala was not surprised to see Manek was already buttoning up the new shirt Antony secured for him, his pants changed. "Is this right, Mr. Pilat?" Manek went over to Antony, who had chosen to take a guard position at the front door.

Realizing the older man was giving her the space Sala needed to maintain her modesty, she looked down at her clothes. These were the same ones she had worn for the last three and a half months. She was sure that the stench from them would linger in this house for a very long time. Her once sturdy light gray wool skirt now looked almost black, covered in the dirt and grime of the ghetto. The fringes were starting to fray and the waist was rolled over two times to hold the skirt up. In another life she would have been embarrassed by the small amount of her knee that was showing, but who had time for useless emotions such as those? She looked over to the clean clothes that sat on the table. They represented hope and determination. They would survive, she would make sure of it, they would all be together again. Sala swiftly changed into her new life.

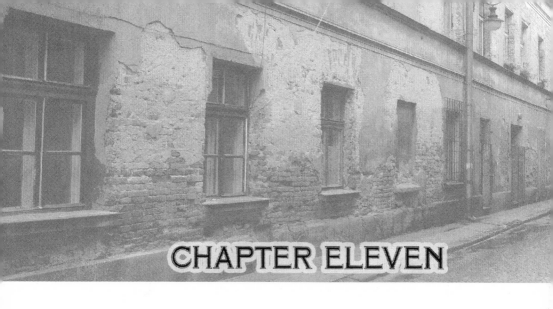

CHAPTER ELEVEN

Manek stood next to Mr. Pilat, trying to understand what he was doing. The older man kept his hand on his shoulder as the two of them stared out into the darkened night cloaking the deserted alley. When Manek tried to turn around to check on Mamusia and Zosia, he wouldn't let him budge an inch. He was going to be nine years old soon. Zosia was only six, still a child. He was a man, though, and men knew how to take care of the women they loved.

"I'm ready."

When the men turned, they saw Sala and Zosia both wearing new dresses, tights and shoes. Antony must have seen how thin they had gotten, and made sure the clothes he got for them were a smaller size. Although Sala had lost much of the curves that had made her a woman, the dress fit nicely around her waist. Zosia looked like a princess in her new dress that fit snugly on her already thinning frame. The children pulled on light coats, grateful for some additional warmth on the cool summer night. Mamusia had her same coat from home, the one with the special pockets she had never mentioned to anyone.

"Good. I will walk out first. I'm going through this door, down the street, and then I will turn a left and keep walking until I leave the city. Sala and Zosia must follow me, staying a few feet behind at all times. Manek, you will follow on your own." Manek's spine straightened at the older man's confidence in him. "You will keep walking. Keep looking straight ahead at all times. Do not look down, do not look away or turn around. Put one foot in front of the other and keep walking. No matter what, none of you should stop for anything. Keep walking," he stressed. "If anyone tries to stop you, just keep going. If they stop me for any reason, pass on by and keep going. Pretend you do not know me. Just keep walking, no matter what."

Manek glanced at his Mamusia and Zosia. They looked scared, so he gave them a confident nod. They could do this. They could do anything as long as they were together.

Plus, escaping the ghetto had to be good for them.

"If you are ready …."

"We shall be fine, Mr. Pilat."

He looked at Manek and smiled. "No matter what …"

"Keep walking," Manek finished for him.

The door opened and closed behind Antony without making a sound. Manek smiled at Zosia, telling her, "You should hold Mamusia's hand in case she gets scared." His little sister smiled at the suggestion and she took their mother's hand.

Sala opened her mouth to say something to him when she got to the door, but he forestalled her. "I'll be right behind you, Mamusia." She nodded, and left as well, Zosia peering at him over her shoulder with worried eyes. They all had seen what the police captain would do to people suspected of escape. They would be shot in the head without question. Or worse, dragged into the center of the street and made into sport for his men. This was the life her children had grown accustomed to in the short time they had stayed in Dembitz.

Manek rested his forehead against the door as he took in a deep breath. One heartbeat. He closed his eyes. Two heartbeats. He opened them and let out his breath slowly. Time to go.

The streets seemed so dark that night. He had only been to Dembitz once before, in daylight, and in the town square, where people were always rushing about. Now, with the streets quiet, and no one around, it felt as if the moonlit shadows were about to come alive.

Manek held his head up high like Poppa, and he kept his feet moving in a steady straight line. He felt as if there were thousands of eyes staring back at him from the shadows, and he lowered his head. Looking down at his shoes, he thought about his father and his shoes. Mamusia had ordered them special for Poppa's birthday just last year. They were shiny, dark leather with special stitching that did little loops over the pointed toes. He was always staring at those shoes, endlessly trying to walk the same way his Poppa did.

When he grew up, he wanted his Mamusia to buy him shoes that were exactly the same. He wondered where those shoes where. What was Poppa doing right now? Why had he not come to find them? When would he? He quickly stopped this train of thought. He had no time for aimless questions. This was not a time for answers. This was a time to escape. He had to keep walking.

He got to the corner and made the turn, as Mr. Pilat instructed. He might not be able to go to school, but Manek knew he was smart. He had learned all kinds of things, and he knew most of all how to follow directions. Far ahead of him, he could see his Mamusia and Zosia. They were walking quickly, but he kept his steady, even pace. Like Poppa used to in his special shoes.

The walk through the town felt like it was taking forever. He felt as if every shadow was filled with the Kapos, ready to jump out and attack him. He was terrified someone would open a window any moment and yell about the Jewish boy walking alone in the middle of the night. He wished he had a hat to wear so no one could see the dark fuzz that covered his head.

One step in front of another. Don't look left. Don't look right. Look straight ahead.

As he took each step, he could feel eyes on his back. Was that just his own imagination, or were people peering through their windows at him?

He wanted to run. It would be so much faster to just run and catch up with the rest of them. But Mr. Pilat was clear. He could not attract any attention. He had to stay strong, and swallow the fear that was threatening to take over. He could do this.

When he came to the last building, he saw the forest ahead of him. He made out Mamusia and Zosia disappearing inside the trees.

Manek hurried his pace just a bit.

He was so close. Once the dark trees would have scared him. He would have waited for Poppa or Uncle David to come with him and protect him. He would have been sure some terror lay in the black shadows that danced around him.

Now Manek knew that the worst nightmares lay behind him in the light.

"This is the Jaworze D. forest," Antony explained to Manek and Zosia. "We have a long walk ahead of us, but at the end is a nice house with a big roomy attic where you three can hide. They have food for you, and you'll be safe. I know it will be hard to make the walk, but—"

"We can do it."

Everyone looked at Zosia in shock at her confident willingness. The little girl stood waiting, eyeing the tall trees around them.

"Zosia—" Sala stopped as her emotions rose up and swept her words away.

"We can do it, sister."

Zosia smiled at him and offered him her hand. They clasped their fingers together and looked at the adults. "Let's go."

CHAPTER TWELVE

Sala came awake with a start. They'd been hiding up here for five months, but it still felt as if all three of them were catching up on their sleep. Being the only ones inhabiting the attic was positively luxurious after months of living in a two-by-six-foot space. In the ghetto, even when they had moved to the first floor of the house that took them in, the space was still limited to the point of suffocation.

Checking on the children, she smiled. While asleep, little Manek kept one hand on his sister. This was her favorite time of the day, when she woke up and saw her children sleeping peacefully.

She retrieved the bucket they all used to relieve themselves and carried it to the ladder. Each night, before the children rose, she would make sure the bucket was emptied. Any chance she had to relieve her children of the discomforts of their new way of life she took with gratitude. This, to her, had become the meaning of being a mother.

"Together," she mumbled to herself. That one word had become her mission, prayer, and plea all combined.

Outside, the countryside was wrapped in deep night. There was snow on the ground, but the owners of this place kept the paths cleared. She assumed they needed to keep the stable path cleared so they could tend their livestock, but she was still surprised at how often they went outside. There were so many footprints everywhere, it felt like an army must be walking around.

Emptying the pail, Sala trudged over to the well and brought up a bucket of water. Filling their waste pail with fresh water, she swirled it around and walked repeatedly between the cesspit and well to make sure their bucket was thoroughly washed out. The only way to keep the attic from stinking to high heaven was this little ritual she had adopted. It struck her as humorous that something her husband would have regarded as beneath her now provided her with a treasured precious few moments for herself.

The act of moving freely around, of breathing clean, fresh air, of being a mother again instead of a hunted victim—this was her second favorite time of her day.

The moon hung fat in the sky. Owls hooted from the trees not far from the house, and a lonely wolf howled in the distance. Good. No planes, automobiles, or marching soldiers. It was safe. Or at least, as safe as they could be. Sala took a few extra moments to use the fresh water to clean her face and hands. A bath was out of the question, something Manek took great delight in teasing her about. She, however, sorely missed the feeling of being thoroughly clean.

Returning to the house, she steeled herself to face the coming night. They had quickly adopted the habit of staying up at night and sleeping during the day. Less chance of being seen. She made the children sleep near a small window in the attic, for this was their only chance of getting sunlight. How would they grow without the sun? Sala thought of the crops her husband used to labor over with such care. He would want his children to grow as strong and tall as his corn.

Shaking herself out of such regrets, she forced herself to consider what they would do tonight. She used the time to come up with something to occupy the children to wile away the hours. A geography lesson, perhaps? Or no, she should keep them focused on their letters and numbers.

Before she went inside, she saw Mrs. Mordel struggling with two large buckets and a lantern. Hurrying over, she put her own pail down. "Are you okay?"

"Yes, yes." The other woman glanced at the barn and then her with worry.

"Can I help? Do these need to go to the barn?" Sala started with surprise when she looked down into the buckets. One was filled with water and the other had loaves of bread wrapped in cloth. She thought she had developed a friendship with this woman, but now it looked like she had some secrets—

"My husband and son haven't returned from their trip. They

usually are the ones who take it."

"Oh. They're heavy. I'm happy to carry one."

"I have a secret," the woman blurted out before realizing what she had said. "You must not ever tell anyone, though."

"Would you like to share it with me?" Sala resisted the urge to point out she had no one to tell secrets to.

Mrs. Mordel nodded her head. "Come with me."

Sala hefted one of the buckets while Mrs. Mordel carried the other. When they got to the barn, the woman slid the door open a crack, wide enough for them to slip through but not so wide anyone could see inside. The barn was dark, so Sala lingered by the door. Mrs. Mordel cautiously waited until the door was fully closed before she lit the lantern. This same caution they took with the attic hatch.

"I'm hiding others," Mrs. Mordel glowed with triumph. "We hide Jews in here, too. It is our way of fighting those Germans."

Sala looked around the empty barn, not understanding what the woman was talking about. The Mordels were good people. They'd provided decent food and the children were beginning to thrive, thanks to their protection. Sala had met their son only once, but she swiftly realized why this gentile family, not Jewish, would care to do what they could for a group of Jews. Their son was mentally disabled. The Germans were quite clear on their stance on anyone deemed imperfect. They were summarily executed or sent away into the deep holes where they put people they wished to forget.

Those holes had many names that people gave them, but Sala knew what they were. Graves.

"Are these invisible Jews?" Sala smiled at her joke, planning on sharing it with Manek later. He was always so serious now. She wanted to put some light back into her little boy's eyes ... wait, no, not a little boy. She had to stop calling him a little boy even in her mind. He deserved more than that.

"I'll show you." Mrs. Mordel whistled softly, three long, plaintive notes. When the last one finished, Sala saw the hay in the loft above them move. The wall in the far corner also shifted, and out emerged ... her cousins.

Sala took several steps forward, until the water sloshing over the side of the pail reminded her to set it down. "What are you doing here?" The anger she felt back in Dembitz returned swiftly to the surface.

"You made it out of Dembitz?" Isaac asked

"How?" Ringel stared at her with suspicion hardening his eyes.

Bunek tilted his head to the side. "Who helped you, Sala? Tell us, now. We won't judge you if you gave the Germans—"

"I am sure it is nothing like that," Isaac quickly inserted. He turned to Sala and smiled. "It wasn't, right? I mean, it couldn't be. We knew your parents and your husband. You would never collaborate."

Sala flinched at the word, shocked speechless that they would dare make such an outrageous accusation. What? Because she was a woman, the only way she could survive was to make a deal with the devil? And the Germans were indeed the living embodiment of the beast to her. A woman, she thought, has more reasons than any man to find a way to survive. They risk their lives to bring new life into the world, and children become your life, heart and soul as soon as you feel that first fluttering deep within you. She survived because of two reasons. Manek and Zosia. This was all they needed to know.

"How did you do it, Sala? Tell us."

"With no help from any of you." She looked at all three of them. "We got here on our own. We are fine, and this is all you need to know." Turning to Mrs. Mordel, she smiled. "Thank you for showing me, but this trio means nothing to me anymore."

Returning to the house, she started to plan what she would teach the children that night. Numbers and letters. Building blocks to knowledge, they must perfect them before she would move them to more complicated subjects. They would count the rocks she smuggled in, and review the letters she was able to form using her fingers.

It was good to learn, for she herself just got the biggest lesson of all. Sometimes, when it is a Mamusia and two children, three was a much mightier number than six.

This was a lesson she would share with them in a different time.

CHAPTER THIRTEEN

Manek stood with Zosia as Mamusia spoke with Mrs. Mordel. A few weeks ago, the farmer's wife had shown Mamusia her hidden cousins in the barn. Now sadness filled the woman's eyes, and all her resolve to fight was gone. As she told Sala the events that had unfolded, all color drained from Sala's face. When the farmer and his son were returning from town, they came across a German patrol. They were always on the hunt for runaway Jews, and suspected that some local Poles were hiding them. Truth be told, it was not only the Jews that were targets. Hitler had determined that the Poles were an obstruction to obtaining enough living space for Germans, so they would use any excuse they had to eliminate both. The soldiers asked the boy, whose mind didn't work right, if he'd seen any Jews. He had. He'd seen Manek and he'd seen two of the men in the barn. When the German soldier demanded an answer, the boy told the truth. He'd seen two and a half Jews the previous night.

The soldier shot Mrs. Mordel's son in the head.

Such a terrible tragedy forced the Mordels to make a decision. They explained that they would no longer be able to hide their Jews. They'd done what they could for them and lost so much in the process. Besides, winter was almost over.

Sala felt her world start to collapse from the inside out. When would the killing stop? How many lives had to be lost? And this one felt like her fault. These kind people had opened their homes and hearts, had helped save her children, and they ended up losing one for their kindness.

To make matters worse, the winter might be over on the calendar, but nobody told Mother Nature. It was very cold, with snow everywhere. And the rainy season was going to start.

She was sure Manek and Zosia would not survive in the forest.

"I do not know the right words to comfort you. You have been so kind and brave, and in the process you lost the one thing you cherish the most. I hate to even ask, and I'm not sure it would matter, but are you sure you will not change your mind?"

Mrs. Mordel shook her head at Mamusia's question. "I cannot. We have lost too much already. Please. I will watch the children while you look for a place, but you must go within a few days. We cannot risk the Germans wanting to check on the *ranting* of a crazy boy."

Sala accepted her defeat. "Thank you for watching the children."

Zosia and Manek both slept away the day while Mamusia went out to find them a new place to stay. Her efforts were rewarded, and she returned by the time the children woke up.

"Come, Manek and Zosia. It is time."

"Where will you go?"

Mamusia turned at Mrs. Mordel's question. "It is best if you do not know. It is safer for you that way." She hugged the woman tightly, and then the three of them began to walk away.

"Where are we going, Mamusia?"

Sala stumbled at Zosia's question but kept them moving. "You remember the Dziedzic family? They live just down the road from our old house. They help Jewish people, and Mrs. Dziedzic made us a nice place to stay."

Manek hid a smile. When Mamusia got the most chipper and positive, he knew it meant they were about to do something they would not enjoy. Not only that, he remembered how long it took to get from home to Dembitz, and then how long the walk was to reach the Mordels. Walking all the way back to the Dziedzic house felt like it would take forever. He wondered if he would get shorter from all the walking. Nevertheless, he resolved to make the best of a bad situation.

"Zosia, what comes after two?"

"Three."

Manek looked down at his feet. "Let's count our steps and see how high we can go. If we don't know the number, we'll have to start it over again. Want to play?"

"Yes," she yelled at the top of her lungs.

Zosia did not notice when both Manek and Mamusia winced at the noise she made. There were no Germans in sight, but such an outburst could possibly attract their attention.

"One," he took a giant step. Mamusia gave him a small smile, one of the few he'd seen in a while, and it made his heart swell in his chest. When his sister gave him a suspicious look, he motioned her to come stand beside him. "We'll make a game out of the numbers Mamusia taught us. We'll walk together and we each have to say a number when we do. Whoever forgets has to start us over at the number one again. Maybe we can count up to this million Mamusia has told us about. Now, I'll try this again." Manek took a step forward. "One …"

* * *

"Two." Sala kept her hands over her two children's mouths as she tried to lie as flat as possible, willing herself and them to mold into the floor, as she felt the German soldiers moving around in the attic, talking to each other. The Dziedzics had been as good as their word. They had put them in the attic of the barn where they stored the hay. When they first entered the attic, the sweet, fresh smell attacked their nose. This hay was freshly cut, and not mixed with the animal manure yet. The hay had filled up almost three quarters of the attic, standing four to five feet deep. Manek and Zosia had regarded the filled space with suspicion, but all she saw was a comfortable, warm spot to wait for the coming summer. Even though the slits through the roof let the cold air in, it couldn't have been a better spot.

Or so she thought.

One day the SS came to make inquiries. The Dziedzic house was close to the road, and the barn right next to it. When Sala heard the trucks pull up outside, she warned the children they had to be silent. Just in case, she took them all to the place farthest back in the attic and then buried them under the piles of hay. The needles pricked their sides, and it was difficult to breathe. But none of that mattered when your life was at stake. She positioned them to each side of her and had put her hands over their mouths. But the hay was so reactive to the slightest movement, she was afraid that if they even breathed heavily, the soldiers would see them.

"Where are the Schonwetters?"

The German demand carried all the way from the house. They are looking for us? Why? Surely, the authorities assumed they were dead and buried. She'd heard the reports of the liquidation in Dembitz. The SS had been ruthless in their pursuit of finding the escaped prisoners as soon as they could. The Dziedics were close family friends that lived a few houses away, but she never thought the Germans would be looking for them anymore. She thought they'd been forgotten within the chaos of the Dembitz deportations.

When they did not find any stowaways in the house, she heard a squadron burst into the barn. In due course they climbed the ladder that led to the attic. As they passed through the small trapdoor leading into her haven, their boots felt like exploding bombs echoing through the small space and making their prone bodies vibrate with the impacts. The Germans loved to do everything loud. She thought she heard the Dziedics below, speaking as fast as possible, but it was all a murmured blur drowned out by her thundering heart.

She imagined the SS, dressed in their gray coats with the shiny buttons, searching all around the small loft. The only thing on this second floor was the abundant amount of hay. There was nothing to see.

Why were they taking so long?

Playing Manek's game, she started counting off the seconds in her head. She could feel her children's breaths against her palms. She lost track of what number she was up to.

"One. Two …"

A metal clang shattered the silence. Pssht, pssht. In her mind's eye she could imagine an SS soldier, frustrated at being assigned a fool's errand, grabbing the pitchfork the Dziedzics kept in the corner and thrusting it into the hay, randomly hoping to hit his mark.

The sounds were getting closer. She tightened her grip on her children, feeling their bodies trembling beneath her hands. She was trapped. There was nowhere to run. She silently prayed to a God she did not think listened, and then entreated the husband she hoped could hear her. Please let them survive this horror.

Her entire body turned to ice as she felt the boots draw near. She tensed her limbs, waiting for impact.

"Please let it be me and not my children that is stabbed," she silently prayed.

As the tip of the pitchfork pierced her leg, her survival instincts took over. She did not move, not even flinch. The pain was masked by the shock of being injured. The tine was pulled out as quickly as it was thrust, and the pitchfork plunged again a few feet away. She finally heard it thrown into the corner of the attic with a clatter. Slowly, softly, Sala let out her breath in relief.

Their footsteps, a sound she had grown an expert at listening for, were descending down the ladder.

Next they heard a truck door open and close.

Sala imagined the Dziedzics following the Germans outside, smiling bravely as the occupiers left without wreaking any major damage. This was all the Polish people could ask for during these murderous times. Indubitably, she and the children would have to leave soon. But moving on might be for the best. She'd come here because they were desperate after Mrs. Mordel had ended their stay. These were good, kind people who had done all that they could.

Asking for more from them, especially after the Germans had searched the house, would only make her feel ashamed.

When they crawled out from underneath the piled hay, the three of them let out breaths so loud they all smiled. They sounded like they had just plowed all of the fields by hand, no help from a horse or plow. Sala steeled herself and she checked her leg. She tried to turn away so she didn't scare the children. She scanned the wound to her thigh. It was no more than a bad scratch, not even much blood drawn. She sent a silent prayer of thanks.

"Mamusia," the children said in unison, pointing at her coat with horrified faces. Looking down, she saw her coat, the one she'd kept with her through so many obstacles and traumas, now bore three pitchfork-sized holes on one side.

"Well," she poked her fingers through the holes and wiggled them at her children, "at least they missed the pockets."

CHAPTER FOURTEEN

"But, Mamusia, where will we sleep?"

"In the forest, of course, Zosia. We will sleep in the forest. The trees will hide us. The ground will give us food to eat, and wood to burn. The streams will provide us water to drink, even to wash in. We are going into the forest."

"But why Mamusia?"

"Our family will be safe with the trees." Always with the questions, her daughter. Manek was more steady. He was his father, through and through. He would take all of the information in and process it in his own way. When he was ready he would understand what the adults knew with far more detail. Zosia wished to know everything now and she was not hesitant to ask for it.

Sala loved her daughter for this trait. She was even more proud she'd given birth to such a strong, smart girl. But she was afraid Zosia's demands would get them all killed.

Zosia was seven years old now. Sala made herself remember what Manek was like when he was that age. She remembered what she was like, as wild as the wind. Always running after her brothers, trying to outdo the boys. She remembered how proud her antics made her grandfather. How he would have adored these children of hers. He would have spent hours with Zosia …

"Why, Mamusia? Why? Why? Why?"

"Enough, child," Sala laughed. "We will go into the woods because there I know we can be safe. One day, when this war is over, we will be able to go wherever we wish, you shall see."

It was late April, and spring had sprung. Although the night was really quite cold, during the day the temperature was above freezing, and the rain seemed to have stopped. She was still stunned by the unselfish, heroic words the Dziedics had spoken as she left. She could remember the look on their faces, the conviction in their voices, when they told her they would continue to help. When winter came again, she could rely on them to assist her in finding shelter. In this dark world, she was slowly finding that bonds of friendship were as powerful as bullets.

She turned to Zosia and continued, "Years ago, before you were born, when I was just around your age, actually … I lived through a war like this."

"Is this what the Germans coming is called? War?"

"Yes, Zosia. This is war. When I was your age, there was a war back then, too."

"Were the Germans here then?"

"No, Manek. When I was little, the Russians invaded our land and they were everywhere. They were mean and cruel."

"Like the Germans?"

"Yes, my smart daughter. Just like the Germans. Your grandma and grandpa taught me to run into the woods when the soldiers came. Run deep into the woods with my sisters and brothers—"

"Uncle David."

Two words. They were all it took to make her stop in her tracks, kneel before her son, and hug him close to her chest. Zosia had already forgotten her uncle, but Manek would remember. She knew no matter what, her son would never forget. Perhaps, for people surviving a war, not being forgotten was the only keepsake one could truly hope for. Being recalled with fondness, with love, would be the best kind of memorial of all, and she could promise David's spirit that much.

She started once more on their trek. As soon as they entered the woods, she felt as if the trees closed around them with a comforting embrace. "Your grandparents taught us all to take to the forest," she said, taking up her story for them again. Talking freely was a nice change after the few weeks they had spent buried in the hay. "Your great-grandfather showed us the things we could eat in the forest. The way to make a fire which emitted no smoke. How to make sure the water we used was pure and clean. In the forest, we can survive without anyone's help."

"This is good," Manek stated. "I don't like us putting people in danger. We're better together, just us."

Sala smiled. Once again, her son understood before most adults. "Children, I will show you how to do all the things your great-grandfather showed me. We will be together and put no one else in danger."

"Until it gets cold."

Again, her son was being far-sighted. She had no idea what they would do when the weather turned again. But for now, while the sun shone brightly in the sky, she would use the outdoors as their shelter.

See our children, Israel? They will grow. They will feel the sun. They will run and learn. They will survive. And they would do all of these things because she would never give up on them. "We will eat and get fat in the forest, wait and see."

"But will you go alone?"

Freezing in their tracks at the sound of a male voice, Sala pushed the children behind her. Isaac, Bunek and Ringel stood in the path. "How did you find us?"

"We followed you," Bunek said.

Isaac smiled at them. "Sala, we are sorry for everything we did before. We've found a group of people in the woods. Some of them we knew from before, and some are from Dembitz. We came to take you to them."

"Why?"

"To make up for not helping you before," Isaac assured her.

Her fingers clenched in the coats on Manek and Zosia as she tried to decide what to do. It would be easier to have some help. More eyes to keep the children together and safe. Strong hands to do some of the work. Perhaps joining a band was a good idea. But her anger at her cousins had not dissipated, even after all this time. Her inner arguments ranged back and forth. On the other hand, anger did not feed an empty belly. She would never forget what they did, but now was not the time to let pride get in the way of survival.

She nodded at last, and silently the three of them followed the cousins through the forest. At the end of their march, she was stunned to come upon a group of almost twenty people. Men, women, and even two other children. Sala let Zosia and Manek go run to meet the new children, the first faces near their age since they had run from Brzostek so long ago.

Yet Sala was not persuaded that there was safety in numbers. "Isaac," the other man bent over so she could whisper in his ear, "there are too many people here. We'll be spotted."

"Nonsense, Sala."

"You are just a woman," Bunek pointed out. "What would you know?"

"Little Sala knows more than you think."

They all turned at the words from this knowing voice. Standing behind them were three men: another cousin, Ignash; Romek, an old friend of Israel's; plus another man she'd never seen before. Sala hugged Ignash tightly. She was so grateful to find a man who knew her, who knew her family, and was not scared to admit he may not be all-powerful. "I can't believe it," she wiped her eyes when they began to tear. "What are you … How are you … I'm so glad you're here."

"We are fine, Sala," Romek said. "This is my friend, Fish." She shook the other man's hands.

Ignash faced off with Bunek and Isaac. "What is this about? You know how smart Sala's grandfather was. He taught her everything he knew, and then her grandmother added to her store of knowledge. If Sala says there is danger, we should probably depart. You are foolish to make the mistake of not listening to her."

"She's just scared. We've been fine here for weeks."

"You've stayed in one place for weeks?" Sala asked Isaac. "We have to keep moving." She immediately looked around for Zosia and Manek.

"We're not moving," Bunek said.

"I'm sorry." As she looked around at the group, her gaze lingered on the other mother. Manek and Zosia would be happy to have some friends.

Then she realized that her son returned to her side when she wasn't looking. He was watching the exchange, his large dark eyes absorbing everything around him. His face revealing no emotion.

"Mamusia, Zosia and I are ready to go when you are."

She took his hand, and his small fingers folded into hers with such trust. She turned back to the men, the men she'd been told since birth she should obey. And she knew that following them was the last thing she should do. Just as she once was forced to raise her hand in violence against her child to save his life, she would now break the mold every Jewish woman was pushed into since the beginning of time. "I am sorry, my cousins. I am willing to forgive you for the past, but I cannot stay here. My children cannot stay here. We have to go."

"Fine," Bunek turned away.

Isaac held a hand out to her. "Sala, we're not coming with you."

She shrugged. "I never asked you to."

Manek ran after Zosia, and Sala knew her son would get her daughter to follow. She saw Ignash, Fish and Romek talking fiercely on the side. Bunek walked away from her in disgust, and Isaac put a hand on her shoulder. "Sala, you are being ridiculous. No one comes out here. The woods are silent."

"So many people will draw attention. They have planes. They have eyes. You will be found. You will die."

"We've been here for weeks with no problem."

"You are going to die, Isaac. Come with me."

"I will not leave my friends. My family."

"And I will save mine." She heard Zosia fussing, and saw Manek furiously debating with his sister.

"That girl will get you all killed."

She did not need this man telling her a thing about her daughter. "She'll learn. Just as you all will."

Ignash joined them once again, and Romek and Fish pulled up behind him with their arms folded over their chests. "Sala—"

"You cannot get me to change my mind."

"I'm not trying to. I'm trying to tell you—"

"We have to go," Sala stated. Striding over to Zosia, she picked her daughter up in her arms. Manek hurriedly joined her as she turned to the group. "I'm sorry, but it is not safe here." All eyes were now on her, wide with disbelief and confusion. "I beg of you all, split up into smaller groups. And leave this place!" She ended almost on a whisper as she begged them to listen. Then she turned to walk away.

When she realized that Ignash, Romek and Fish were all following her, she came to a halt. "You can't stop me."

"I would never try such a thing," Ignash held up his hands in surrender.

Romek smiled. "We're going to come with you."

CHAPTER FIFTEEN

Something is wrong. Sala came awake as fast as a thunderbolt. Not that she showed any sign of it outwardly. She stayed frozen as she tried to determine what had woken her from a sound sleep. It had been chilly last night, she made the children sleep on each side of her so she could gather them close to her body and impart to them a bit of warmth. The comforting beat of their hearts under her palms reassured her. Two heartbeats, moving almost in synch with each other. Her children were peacefully sleeping.

What was wrong?

The crack of a breaking branch pierced through her like a gunshot. The breath froze in her lungs. Slowly she moved her hands so they were positioned to cover her children's mouths if she needed them to stay silent. Turning just her head, she looked across the clearing, only to see Ignash, Romek and Fish fast asleep.

Why wouldn't they listen? She kept telling them they had to keep a watch.

Straining with every fiber of her being, Sala tried to pinpoint where the sound came from. The forest was misleading, though. Sound could bounce around the trees to mislead you.

It had to be coming from a few meters to the west.

Letting out her breath, she slowly slipped free of the comforting warmth of her sleeping children. She tucked her shawl, which they used as a blanket, more tightly around them to keep them warm. Her shawl and her coat, the only two things she managed to keep with her from home. Looking around the dark forest, she sighed in relief. The intruder must have passed without noticing them. At least the men had listened to her decree they couldn't have a fire at night.

Moving to a stump conveniently situated next to a tree, she took a seat, leaned back, and prepared to keep watch.

Come morning, she stayed on her perch as she watched the others rise and start to go about their morning business.

"Mamusia." Zosia soon came over to her with the skirt of her dress drawn up to make a bowl. "Are these all right?"

She glanced down to check what her daughter had picked. "You are getting very good at this, Zosia. All of those mushrooms are safe, and," she snatched a fat berry from the mix, "these are delicious."

The little girl went to a nearby log to sit down and apportion her bounty. She had gotten so thin. The dress she had put on that night they escaped the ghetto now hung loosely on her frail frame. It was a pleasant reprieve to have her occupied counting and sorting berries, as opposed to the constant crying and whining they were used to. They were all hungry, but the small child's endless rants on the subject were constantly getting on the already fragile nerves of the men.

Her grandparents had taught her so many lessons all those years ago. She never imagined that she would put them to such good use. Learning how to live off the land was much different than she had imagined. The days were consumed with one desire, hunting and gathering food. Their lives revolved around these daily activities, and all the while, they had to keep an ear and eye out for anything remotely suspicious or out of the ordinary. It had seemed like a romantic fairy tale all those years ago. Now it had turned into a hopeless, never ending nightmare.

The first thing Sala had taught her children was how to pick edible berries and mushrooms. The next was to never leave her sight. She was constantly concerned they would have to suddenly flee any unexpected danger, so they needed to stay close at all times. Each had learned how to cope with their new way of living in their unique way. Zosia would collect the food, and carefully lay out portions on leaves for everyone as if she were having a tea party. Manek would straighten where they were, placing twigs in piles where they could use it for the fire or moving branches out of their sleeping area. "Manek." Her son stopped what he was doing and looked at her. "Don't worry about straightening up, son. We won't be staying here any longer. Go and eat with your sister."

"What is this about, Sala?" Romek asked as he stretched and rose from his bed of leaves.

"We're moving to a new spot."

"Not again." Fish took the leaf filled with berries Zosia had made.

"We just moved, I thought." Ignash threw a berry up in the air and caught it in his mouth, making the children giggle. Sala could not help but smile. Her children's laughter had become more precious to her than the jewelry and documents she had stashed in the depths of her coat.

"I know all of this, gentlemen. But last night I heard the sound of footsteps nearby. We have to move. I will not take any chances with the children."

"Here we go again." Romek headed off into the bushes, shaking his head.

"It could have been an animal."

She shook her head at Ignash's suggestion. "It was not. At this point, I know the difference between an animal and human footsteps. We must be going."

"Let's just do it to keep her happy."

Sala ignored Fish's muttered comment, along with the looks of bored resignation on the men's faces. At least her son had the good sense to be happy at the prospect of the change.

Soon they were on their way, heading east. Sala was determined to put a day's march between them and the noise she had heard the night before. While walking they collected food. The gathering was almost a subconscious reaction now. The fruits and mushrooms were good, but they never seemed to fill up anyone. Unless one of the men procured food from a farm, they were constantly on the hunt for something to eat. Fortunately, Manek did not ask what the difference was between procuring and stealing, since that was a question for which his Mamusia did not have the answer.

When they finally chose a new site for a camp, dusk was settling in among the trees. Manek immediately set to work. First, he led Zosia into the trees to collect the dry wood they would use to make a fire. They soon had assembled an untidy stack of angular limbs. He then sent Zosia out to look for food, and he began to pile up leaves for each of them to use that night to sleep.

"None for me, Manek." They all turned with surprise in Romek's direction. "What? I am going into the village tonight."

The young Polish girl he had met in the nearby village was a distraction he was not willing to forgo. Men had their needs, after all.

"It would be better if we stayed together."

Romek gave her a teasing wink at her protest. "And yet ..."

"Being a man, you cannot resist a night with your sweetheart," Sala muttered.

"When you are a man, Manek, try not to fall in love with a shrew like your mother." Romek smiled at her too-serous boy.

"Actually, Manek, I suggest when you become a man, you not act like Romek."

"Got it," her son nodded. "When I'm a man, I won't be an idiot, Mamusia."

They all laughed.

"If you are going anyway, please try to find some potatoes. We could use the food."

Sala turned away as Romek and Fish started to make their way through the trees, heading to the village. At least moving camp had brought them closer to their sweethearts. It meant they would be gone for less time.

"Catch me, Manek!"

Zosia hollered her command as she went running through the trees.

"Hush, Zosia, not so loud, please."

"Yes, Mamusia."

Sala returned to making the fire, and Zosia went back to calling taunts to her brother as she ran around. It was rare to see her child run these days. She had become so weak and frail. At least she had stopped crying for a few moments.

"Zosia, you must be quieter," Manek said.

Once Sala had the fire blazing, she stood up and announced, "I will go and get us some water and make tea. You two stay by the fire and get warm. Manek, remember what to do if you hear anyone approaching."

"I will, Mamusia."

A brief nod was all it took for her to communicate what she had realized their first night in the forest she no longer had to say. Don't be seen. Watch your sister. Be careful near the flames. Don't make noise.

Manek had become her rock. She could depend on him always to understand that their lives depended on staying alert.

If only she could teach her daughter the value of heeding her warnings.

She found a stream not far from where they had stopped. In the distance Sala could still see the huddled forms of her children around the fire. Returning to the camp, she didn't have to go far to find the leaves to make the tea. At least conditions for the natural bounty that grew all around them were good this year. If they hadn't been, they would not have survived. The tea would help the children feel full before the men returned from town with more substantial fare than mushrooms.

When Ignash came to the fire, he watched her bed the children down as he silently drank the tea from their communal cup. The old tin cup had been a special treat that the men brought back from one of their first nights out looking for more substantial food. They took it everywhere they went now, a symbol of a more civilized time. Once she settled next to him, he motioned to Zosia with his head: "I could hear her distinctly."

"She was just playing."

"Loudly, Sala. She plays loudly. She cries loudly. She can barely walk anymore, she is so weak, and when she does, she walks through the forest loudly. Little Zosia does everything we do as loud as she can."

"All eight-year-olds are loud, Ignash."

"You are the one who taught us that being loud will get us all killed."

"I know." She took the cup from his hand and filled it for herself.

"The danger—"

"Hasn't touched us yet, and until it does, I will not abandon my child."

"I fear it will be too late for us when you are ready, Sala."

She bridled at the suggestion that she would ever be ready. "Are you under the impression this decision is up to you?"

He smiled at the affront in her voice. "No, Sala. They are your children."

"They are. And I will decide when and if other arrangements must be made for Zosia. I will take the first watch, get some rest."

Sala settled down where she could rest and still keep an eye on the camp. The state of watchfulness they'd had to adopt when they took to the forest was a constant burden to her. At all times a checklist ran through her mind. Where are the children? Is there anything to eat? Do I see anyone coming? What are the children doing? Any noises jumping out at you?

And always … what are we going to do when it gets cold?

Romek and Fish returned far earlier than their usual time—dawn had not even arrived. Their shadowed expressions put her instantly on guard. She didn't have to do more than kick Ignash's foot to wake him up. He would want to hear this, too.

"Tell me."

"There was a wedding in the village tonight. Almost everyone seemed to be in attendance," Romek said.

"So why has this brought you back so early?" Sala asked.

"I didn't think it was wise to stay."

"Explain," Ignash ordered.

Romek glanced at Fish, and he was the one who took up the story. "The men got very drunk, and there must have been some kind of feud between the bride's and groom's families, because they started to fight."

"Why did this concern you?"

Fish shrugged at Sala's question. "The whole village, all the men, were fighting, Sala. We decided there were too many eyes watching us. Then we heard some of the women calling for the police to break up the fight."

Ignash was alarmed by that news. "It's good you managed to escape."

"Yes . . ." Fish and Romek again shared a look that made Sala uncomfortable, but they didn't elaborate.

"I guess I am awake." Ignash came and sat down on the log next to Sala. "So I will start my turn at watch now."

Sala settled down next to Zosia. She put her arm over her daughter so her hand could rest on Manek's shoulder. Matching her breathing to that of her children's, she soon found herself coasting on a relaxing wave which sent her into a deep state of meditation. Sleep was a luxury they could no longer afford, like new clothes or a roof to sleep under. They didn't need luxuries, though, just each other.

Boom.

Boom, boom, boom.

The retorts sounded like whiplashes across her senses. Sala sat straight up, fully awake. Gunfire. This time there was no question about what was disturbing her sleep. No matter how long it had been since she heard the terrifying explosion of gunfire in the ghetto, the noise was written into her soul.

One that would never be erased.

Fish came awake on his own, and reached over to jostle Romek. Ignash stood leaning against a tree, vainly searching the darkness for an explanation. The full moon would either work against them or for them, Sala wished she had some kind of magical talent to tell which it would be.

Romek sat up on his pallet. "It must be the police. I told you the villagers were going to call them to break up the fight."

"Get up," Fish ordered him.

"Those shots are nearby." As Sala woke up Zosia, Manek was already rising and moving to her other side. "You know I can tell how far the noise is. I have not been wrong before—"

The *rat-tat-tat* of machine gun fire made a cold sweat break all over her body.

"We all know what that means," Ignash told Romek.

"Not the police." Police did not carry machine guns. The SS did.

The children huddled close to Sala while Romek started to grab things from around his pallet. "Let's go. We must run."

"Away from the gunfire."

"No." Sala's commanding voice froze all three men. "We must go toward the gunfire."

"Ah, you've lost it, woman," Romek said.

Fish shook his head. "We cannot. Think of your children."

"I am." Sala squeezed the children tighter to her side. "If someone was walking around out here earlier, they know where we are. They will be expecting us to try to flee. We must out-think them. If we run toward them, but go around where the gunfire is, we will get away. They will never expect it."

The men exchanged looks. The ploy was dangerous, but it did make sense.

"Fine," all three said, nodding.

Sala took the lead, the three men following behind her. They'd adopted the habit of letting Sala go first, walking in her footsteps to avoid breaking any branches and calling attention to themselves. The children stayed behind their mother, their little fists clutching the hem of her coat.

Manek kept his breath slow and even, always using his nose and never his mouth. He could be quieter that way. Zosia's eyes were as big as the moon in her face, and he wished he could hold her hand. Mamusia was very clear, though. They were to hold her coat at all times, they were to follow in her footsteps and they must not, under any circumstances, make any noise.

The gunfire seemed as distant as thunder at first. He had learned in the ghetto what this heralded, though: a storm of death. Even Zosia knew they needed to escape from the danger.

Alternating between walking and a fast jog, Sala kept them moving. He knew she was steering them around the area where they thought the Germans were. He hoped his Mamusia was right. He did not want to die. He wasn't even ten years old yet.

CHAPTER SIXTEEN

When they got to a twisty path, like the one Manek often dreamed about taking Antony Pilat's bicycle down, Mamusia froze. Crouching down behind two large trees, she peered around one edge. As she looked back at all of them, Manek could see the fear starkly twisting his Mamusia's features. She almost seemed like a stranger. She made some hand gestures to the men which they nodded in understanding to. Zosia opened her mouth to ask Mamusia a question, but Manek clapped his hand over her lips in time. He shook his head frantically, and the tears in her eyes only made him feel a little bad.

Don't be seen.

Know where the Germans are.

Manek knew without asking that the Germans were right up ahead. He closed his eyes, trying, for once, to not feel his heartbeat. It was beating so hard he feared the Germans would hear him.

Without saying a word, Mamusia suddenly picked him up. He opened his eyes in surprise, locking gazes with Zosia, who was tucked under Mamusia's other arm, like they were each a bag of potatoes. As Mamusia dashed across the twisty path, her feet as nimble as a deer, Manek had enough time to see the gray coat on the back of a soldier, holding a long, dark gun over his shoulder. Behind Mamusia, he could see the other men— Ignash, Fish, and Romek—following.

Once they dashed inside the trees on the other side of the path, Mamusia put him down and firmly took his hand. Machine gun fire and the single retorts of a rifle suddenly broke out, sending an electric jolt through their entire party. Mamusia kept Zosia in her arms, and the two of them ran as fast as they could. Zosia's hands were clenched so tightly around Mamusia's neck, her little knuckles stood out like snow against the dark coat she wore.

His mother kept them moving as fast as the wind for what felt like hours. His breath began to come out in huge gasps from his mouth. He could hear the adults breathing hard as well, so he hoped the sounds of his labored breath was lost in the midst of the others.

At last Mamusia allowed them to stop. He collapsed where he stood. Zosia came over to him and sat close by. The stain of tears on her once rosy cheeks had dried. The two of them braided their fingers together, as they silently watched what the adults would do now.

Mamusia draped her shawl over them and walked over to a stone to sit down. Fish and Ignash collapsed onto the ground, as their chests still heaved to catch their breath. Romek sat on a stump, his head falling forward as if he had a great weight on his back he could no longer hold.

"Are we far enough?" Fish asked.

"It is over a mile. I think this is enough."

The men nodded at Sala's statement as if they were conferring and not just taking orders from her. Romek was serious and gloomy as he said, "I apologize if I brought this down on us."

"You didn't."

When Romek looked at Sala with a dubious eye, she shook her head.

"They were already looking for us. I heard them the night before the wedding, remember?"

"Right," he said, sounding relieved. "Still, I shall take the first watch."

Romek headed to a small rise, crouched by a tree, and peered out over the dark forest, looking for signs of danger. Manek didn't feel tired. Between the moving to a new place so fast, and then having to run for their lives, and then actually seeing a soldier so close ... sleep was the last thing he felt he could do.

***

Manek was irritable the next day. They had to find food, gather wood, and he had to move the debris out of their way to clear the camp. Mamusia made him take a nap, and he slept so long that when he did not want to sleep that night, she wasn't surprised. He lay down with Zosia so she would sleep, though his gaze was trained on the adults. The men had a heated discussion in a huddle far away from his Mamusia, until she finally demanded to know what was wrong.

"Idiots," Ignash swore and stomped away from them. He took the designated watch position.

"What are you two going to do now?" she asked.

"Sala," Romek said, "I have to go. I have to see what happened."

"He wants to check on his girl."

"We had friends in that village," Romek reminded Fish. "Yes, we should check on all of them, and the others. I have to go and see just what happened after we left. I want to know what we missed."

"You missed a bullet to the head."

Romek flinched as if Mamusia's words had hurt him. "I am sorry. I do not wish to bring danger for us. But if I don't go and see what happened, what kind of man will I be?"

"What kind of people will any of us be with the Germans here?"

"I don't know, Sala. All I know is ... I wish to be the type of man worth saving."

"Go," Sala ordered. "See what you must see. Just make sure no one sees you come back."

CHAPTER SEVENTEEN

Sala was glad Manek had finally fallen to sleep. She knew it wouldn't be easy for him to rest after all the turmoil of the night before. Tucking the shawl up around his chin, she checked both of her children. They would have to move tomorrow. This camp site was too far from any water source and too open to the wind. She was so tired of crouching down behind a tree each time she heard a crackle or felt the unearthly impression of someone watching. Sometimes she felt a hole in the ground would be more comforting than constantly fearing that a shadow would manifest into a German.

A few hours passed before Ignash gave the signal that the men returned. The two men were drinking from the pail they somehow remembered to bring along the previous night. They sat down across from her, but they did not say a word.

"What happened?"

Romek shook his head grimly.

Fish said, "We need to move away from here."

"Away from this place," Romek added.

Sala looked between them in surprise. "We can go back to where we were the night before—"

"No," Romek quickly stopped her.

"It would be best if we not go that way." Fish didn't look at her, he just kept his eyes closed and head down.

"Why?" Ignash asked. "What are you not telling us?"

The three men began to argue and talk as only brothers could. Romek and Fish continued to refuse saying what they had seen. For his part, Ignash would not let it go. Back and forth it went, until Sala found herself retreating from what was being said as she tried to decide what she wanted.

Sala knew why they had come back so shaken—they had seen the reason for the gunfire the night before—and she couldn't stand not knowing. She kept thinking about the woman and two young children from that first group of people they had found in the woods. She pictured her cousins, who she was never quite sure how she felt about anymore. She knew she couldn't trust them, but she had forgiven them, and they were family. There were precious few people she could call that anymore. After all the gunfire the night before, had the group been able to escape it? She was afraid she knew the answer.

"I have to go."

Everyone looked at her with surprise.

"If you will not tell us what you saw, you will have to show us. I need to go and see who survived. I need to see what they did. I will never be able to explain any of this to the children if I do not know how to explain it to myself."

"No ..." Fish said.

Romek held up his hand. "I will take you, Sala. You will not appreciate me taking you when you see the horror for yourself, though. I fear you will hate me for it, actually. I will take you so you can explain it to yourself. Perhaps then, you will be kind enough to explain it to me as well. I just have one request to make. The children should stay here."

"Fine." Sala stood and waited to see who would lead.

Fish gestured to the sleeping forms. "I'll stay with them. I have had enough of such savagery for a lifetime."

"I'll go with you." Ignash rose and joined them.

They walked through the woods in silence: Romek, Sala and then Ignash. Romek's head kept swiveling around, his eyes keenly watching the shadows.

His being cautious for their safety was a nice change.

As they got closer to the scene, Sala could tell something awful lay ahead. Romek, their resident "bandit," the one that would face anything, was tensed up. It was as if he was preparing himself to be assaulted.

The smell greeted them first. It resembled burnt meat. Such a brutal crime she had not considered since she was a young girl. The stench of burned flesh was added to the smell of cooked hair and fabric. The combined aroma burned her nose on the way in and clawed at the back of her throat. She kept swallowing hoping to keep down the contents of her stomach. This piquant sensation she knew would still be fresh on the day she died, no matter if that occurred in the next hour or in forty years. She could only hope the smell was the worst. When they stepped around the last trees, though, Sala realized she was wrong. These were not people she was seeing. Some hunters must have slaughtered their kill on the spot, not caring about the mess and debris they left behind. Her brain was slow to put together the pieces she was witnessing into a coherent picture.

All around her lay bodies. Or, more correctly, pieces of bodies.

They were everywhere.

Ignash fell to his knees, retching out the meager rations they managed to acquire that day. Romek turned his body away from the carnage.

She could not help looking for faces.

In front of her, in a pile of dead leaves, sprawled the body of the little girl Zosia had played with briefly that afternoon, so long ago. But instead of laughing and running around, this child had half of her face missing. The Germans must have shot them first, then turned the machine guns loose on the bodies. Limbs were blown all over the clearing, including an arm hanging from a branch.

Death. Nothing but the most abject slaughter.

The Germans had come and taken away the safety of their ordinary lives. They took their rights. Their homes. Their husbands, brothers, fathers, sons. Taking the lives of innocents was inevitable. She just never imagined that at the same time they would also show no signs of decency. Where was a soldier's honor when civilians were first murdered and then ripped apart by needless machine gun fire?

On the other side of the little girl she spotted her cousin, Bunek. Or at least what was left of him. Ringel would be confident and dismissive no longer. She saw the fat bullseye of the bullet hole between his eyes; the rest of his body must be somewhere else. Amid the barbarous killing ground another smell in the miasma assaulted her senses. When people were shot, their bowels released.

Honor truly was no longer alive in Galicia.

They walked back to their camp in a daze. Ignash was sick, his face slick with sweat. Romek was shaking, his eyes haunted holes, as if he would never see the world the same way again. Sala avoided them both, moving at a brisk pace to get back to her children. She desperately needed to see her kids.

When she got there, she fell to her knees and gathered them close to her chest.

Fish just nodded when they returned and lay down on his pallet.

Ignash wordlessly took the watch. When Romek moved to stop him, he shrugged him off. "What do you think? I will sleep after viewing the work of demons?"

So Ignash took watch. Romek picked a different pile of leaves and lay down.

Breathing slowly and deeply, Sala gently lifted the shawl back so she could see Manek's and Zosia's faces. She felt unworthy, for some reason, of touching them. Dirtied by what she had seen. They were safe. Zosia was crinkling her nose in her sleep. Manek's eyes moved back and forth beneath his eyelids.

They were here. They were safe. They were together.

And perhaps that would be enough to erase the image of Zosia's young friend's ravaged face from her memory.

CHAPTER EIGHTEEN

The next day, their latest flight began. They did not discuss the massacre. They broke camp, and each of them was forced to put away the memory, hopefully never to revisit it again. But a shadow had been cast on their souls, and they could not escape from that darkness. Unfortunately, for Ignash, Romek and Fish, that darkness ignited a fresh wave of anxiety in Zosia. In the worst kind of way.

Sala recognized the men were filled with fear. She understood being afraid—she was terrified. But it was not Zosia's fault. She was a little girl. She was getting so weak she could barely keep up. She cried all the time now.

"You must stay quiet!"

Zosia bottom lip quivered, and she only started to wail louder.

Visions of the night before flooded Sala's eyes. Blood, limbs, the body of the small girl Zosia had played with, all attacking her senses at once. She could not let her child end up like that. Was she punishing her unnecessarily in her futile attempt to keep them together? Would it be justified if they all died together in another slaughter? Could she somehow save her daughter?

They had been hiding on the outskirts of their village, and she was blessed to have Antony and Heniek find them with rations and bits of news or rumors. They had been coming once a week in the beginning, but Antony's visits had started to become more rare. Many times Heniek would come in his place. It had been a couple of weeks, but with the events of the night before, she knew they would come and check on them. The unwavering support and friendship they had extended was about to be tested but again.

Sala looked around and saw the murderous expressions on her friends' faces. She could not delay any longer. "I have decided. The next time Antony or his son-in-law Heniek comes, I will go with them. Manek, however, will be staying with us," she stated firmly. Before they could protest, she held up a hand. "One of them will come soon. I know it. Possibly even tonight."

She spent the rest of the day cuddling her daughter. Manek silently watched her every move, and she knew her son sensed a terrible change was about to come.

His eyes, so like his father's, pierced his mother's heart.

Antony came that night, as Sala had predicted. Even though his visits had gotten more sporadic as time went on, thankfully, tonight it was her old friend.

She had warned him that she might have to take this step. Antony, as was his way, had sworn he would find a place for her daughter should she have to do it. He brought them potatoes and some bread. Each time the elder Pilat came, she felt like she could breathe a little easier for a few hours. Knowing people in the world still remembered them, cared about helping their neighbors, was often the only bulwark that kept her from becoming lost in despair.

People like Antony Pilat, like Heniek, like the Dziedics, they were the only light in this oppressive darkness.

This time, however, his coming only filled her with hopelessness.

Since Zosia was asleep, and the night sky was getting light, she knew she could no longer wait. As she gathered up her child in her arms, Fish assured her he would take care of Manek. "Antony." He stopped talking to Ignash to turn to her in surprise. "I will walk with you part of the way back."

"You do not have to …"

"I know. I just want to. There is something we must discuss."

The walk through the forest was torture to her. In her arms was the girl she loved more than her own self. Now she was sending Zosia away to an unknown fate.

"Are you well, Mrs. Schonwetter?"

"I am resigned, Mr. Pilat. But surely, at this point, we can call each other by our first names?"

Antony stopped and looked at her in the moonlight, his features lined with confusion. "I only seek to give you the proper respect. How are you, Sala? How is little Manek? Not so little anymore, I see."

"Manek is fine."

"What can I do for you?"

"Is there a family with whom you can lodge Zosia for a while?"

He was at first taken aback that the time had come, but he could not be too surprised. He answered hesitantly, "I will find a way. Are you sure this is the right thing to do?"

"How could it possibly be?" She took a shuddering breath. "It is wrong, but . . ."

"It is all you can do." Antony had tears in his eyes. "She needs to go someplace safe. I know a family, the Kowalskis, they are poor but have a few other children. She will disappear in their midst. I will tell them that she is my relative. Zosia will have enough to eat, people who care for her. You cannot do anything else, Sala. You must let me hide her."

Sala shook her head, her hands tightening on Zosia's frail body. "If she was staying with you and your family ..."

"The Germans still come every week to the homestead looking for you. The family they put in your home would inform them if a new child came to live in my part of the house. Nor will your Zosia," he touched a single finger to Zosia's white blonde hair, "fit in with my brood. She will be noticed. Plus, Captain Zeidler still resides nearby, and he would notice. These people, the Kowalskis, will take in your Zosia."

"I don't know how I'll ever repay you for everything you've done."

"It is only what is right."

Zosia stirred in her arms and sleepily looked up at her. "Mamusia?"

"My daughter, Mr. Pilat is here. Isn't that nice?" Zosia turned her head and gave Antony a sleepy smile. "Zosia," Sala waited until her child gazed up at her again. "Mr. Pilat wants to take you someplace safe. Some place you can run and play. Where they will feed you and keep you safe."

"With Manek?"

"No, my love. This adventure, Zosia, you must go on your own."

Antony waited until she had kissed Zosia's cheek before he took her out of her arms. Zosia, still coming out of her sleep, hesitantly went into his arms, tears beginning to well in her eyes. Sala pulled out a small gem stone she had pried from a brooch she kept hidden. "Give them this when you take her to them. Make sure they understand there will be more, but only if they treat her well."

"I swear it, Sala."

She watched them leave, her heart pounding in her chest like a trapped bird beating viciously against a window to be free. When she could no longer make out their forms through the gloom, Sala returned swiftly to the camp. Manek. She had to go and hug Manek. She had to feel his heartbeat, strong and true under her palm.

Yet she had gone only halfway before she had to stop. Crouching down, both of her hands over her mouth, she let the sobs that had been building up break free. Her entire body convulsed with the force of her grief, and she had to hold onto a tree to stay upright. What did she just do? How could she have? She'd given up her child. How could she give away her daughter? What kind of mother does such a thing? How could she not, though? She ... what would her husband think? What would David say?

She hadn't even let Manek know before she sent his sister away.

Pressing her face into the bark of the tree, she held onto it as if it were a life preserver to save her from a storming sea. Her thoughts kept racing: They were not together. She's promised they would stay together.

What was there to fight for anymore?

* * *

When she returned, dawn was almost breaking. Her eyes were swollen from crying and her throat burned from all the dry heaving she had done. She felt like a golem, a demon, little more than a lifeless shell. But wasn't that what she was? Only a monster could give away their own child. She had made a promise to herself, and now she had broken it. Her honor was all she had left, and even that was now stained.

She found Manek sleeping soundly, and she did not have the heart to even go lie down next to her son. What would she say? How could she explain to him where Zosia went, when she herself could not even believe what she had done?

Ignash sat leaning against a tree. It was his night to keep watch.

"Sala..."

"Don't say a word." Her voice cracked, but she would not break down in front of these men. She would be strong.

"It had to be done. I know how hard it was for you."

"You know nothing! How could you? Is it your child you gave away? How could you possibly know how I feel?" Her voice started to tremble. She had to get control of herself. She took a deep breath. "No, I am sorry to have snapped at you. I know she will be well taken care of, Antony promised. I just hope that one day she will be able to forgive me." Even though I will never be able to forgive myself, she thought.

Their raised voices seemed to wake up the rest of the men. Manek started to stir.

"Mamusia? Are you okay?"

"Yes, my sweet child, how did you sleep?"

Manek looked next to him, and then back to his Mamusia.

"Where is Zosia? I did not feel her get up this morning."

The men all stared at Sala, no one daring to make a sound.

"She went on a little trip with Antony. I took her last night."

"When will she be back?"

"I am not sure, but it will be soon, don't worry."

"But why didn't we all go? And why did she leave without saying goodbye?"

All the questions, she knew they would come, but her head hurt her so much. Manek never asked questions, and she did not know how to answer, so she just stared back at her smart young boy. He had been a crutch for her, and now he seemed like such a small, fragile child. He was all she had left.

He was all she had left, because she gave away her daughter.

"It will all be okay. It just happened so fast, and we did not want to wake you. Please Manek, it will all be OK." She did not know what she was saying anymore.

Thankfully, Ignash intervened. "Come, Manek, let's go find some berries for breakfast."

The other men also started to scramble around, no one looking Sala in the eye. It was just as well. She needed to sit for a moment and gather herself. Just a moment.

She lay down and closed her eyes, but she felt she would never truly sleep again.

* * *

She got through the day. Manek didn't ask questions about Zosia. Somehow, her incredibly smart boy figured out that wherever his sister had gone was destroying his Mother. Sala moved as she should. She kept watch. She gathered food with her son. She tried to wash their clothes when it was especially warm. She sat by the fire as the men told Manek stories to spend the hours.

And yet, deep inside, she grieved.

Sala didn't know you could walk and talk and move and eat and yet, feel nothing but sorrow. Losing Israel hadn't even affected her so deeply. Her arms felt empty. Her heart felt pained, each beat a belabored action of a dying organism.

The sun was no longer bright. The wind was cold. The stars were dull as viewed by her tired eyes.

Though the men went out to get them food, Sala knew it was her instincts that were keeping them alive. She was the one who chose their camp site. She was the one who remembered where they had been so where they should go next. She was the one who directed Manek on how to forage so they could supplement the meager potatoes the men retrieved from dark fields in the middle of the night. The potatoes were getting smaller and full of eyes. Whatever was happening outside of the safety of the trees was as bad as what was happening inside her heart.

She had to keep going. They had to keep going. She just didn't want to without her precious daughter.

* * *

Weeks turned into months. Time had passed and yet it seemed that it was standing still. Fall was approaching. Luckily, the forest had remained quiet after the massacre, but no one could be sure that they would not encounter a Nazi patrol at any moment.

The men made constant pointed remarks about hiding from the Nazis being quieter and simpler without Zosia. Yet Manek's wide dark eyes kept looking at her with hurt, even a little fear. He had come to realize that this "little trip" was much more than his Mamusia had first said. Did he wonder if she would send him away next? Or was he just afraid, wondering what was happening with his little sister?

At the beginning he would keep asking her when Zosia would return. After a while he stopped asking. She caught him, four or five times a day, turning to talk to Zosia or to call her to him.

Yet Manek's silent censure wasn't the worst. The worst part was the way her arms felt so empty.

At night, when she woke up from another nightmare, and reached for the heartbeats … she could only count to one.

Nightmares were a constant problem. She kept seeing the massacre scene, but now, rather than the nameless woman's daughter, it was her own child's face. Zosia, her features streaked with blood, a gaping, burned hole in the middle of her eyes. Night had become as much an enemy as the Germans. The nightmares felt more like foreboding, she knew something was horribly wrong. She woke with a start.

"Manek …"

"Mamusia? What is wrong?"

"I think …"

"Go and get her." How intuitive and smart he was, she thought, her little young man.

The next night Antony came, as he did sporadically each week. "Zosia," she rushed over to him with Manek in tow. "Please, Antony. You have to get my girl."

"Are you sure?"

"Right now. Please."

"Has something happened?" He glanced down at the boy.

"No. I just … I cannot live without my Zosia. I cannot explain it, but I feel like I must go to her, she needs me."

He nodded. "Then I will go now. It will be a long walk, but I can make it there by the morning."

"We will come part of the way with you."

"Of course."

The first hour they walked in silence. She ignored the memory of the dark expressions on the three males' faces they left behind when they realized where she was going. She walked with the gladness that Manek's happy expression gave her. He was so excited, he had a skip in his step. As they walked, Sala kept mulling over something in her mind. She appreciated the steady calming presence Antony had. His deferential manner reminded her that she was the wife of an important man, and not how she was now, little more than a wanted criminal with a bullseye on her forehead. "Antony, I have thought about it. I think it is only right. It is what Israel would want."

"What would Israel want, Sala?"

"He would want you to have the house. The one on the side acreage. The land is good, and if you put your mind to it, you could make a good life there. Israel would want you to have that house. I know it is smaller than ours—"

"It is a virtual palace, Sala. But you do not have to do this. I do not do this for money, or for reward. I do it out of honor and loyalty. I would never expect anything in return."

Sala smiled. No, he would never ask. That humility only made her want to do it more. It also assured her that giving him the house was the right thing. "I know this, Antony. It is what my husband would have wanted. You should have that house and farm. If this war ever ends, and we are still alive, I swear I will sign the deed over to you."

"This is most kind of you, Sala. But again, that is not the reason I am helping you."

Dawn broke over the countryside, and for the first time Sala could see what the war had done to the farms in the area. There would be famine. The crops were abandoned or the fields not sown. There were few animals, and what cattle she could see were gaunt. The Nazis took Poland to feed their army. But they did not know how to farm, nor did they care to. They did not understand the importance of being caretakers of the earth. And now the soil was turning on them. If the world had forgotten the Polish people, at least the soil was proving its independence and showing the Nazis what you sow when all you plant is hatred.

As they slowed before one farm, she took note that rather than dawn heralding the call to work for the men on this place, no one emerged from the main farmhouse at the rooster's crow. Either these people were lazy, or they no longer felt any reason to bother caring for the land. Israel always said you had to take care of the land so the land would take care of you.

As they approached the house, she stopped and waited deep in the forest for Antony to retrieve her precious Zosia.

Time seemed to stand still. He was gone for what seemed like hours. What was taking him so long? When she finally heard the rustling in the trees, she anxiously stood up, with her heart beating so fast she felt it would explode in her chest.

Antony appeared, but not with her daughter. He had brought a small little boy, whose shaved head made him look like a wrinkled bean. The boy had stopped short in the small clearing.

"Antony, where is she?" Sala said in despair.

He returned to fetch the young emaciated child. He walked toward her, looking down at his feet, hiding the tears in his own eyes. He had to swallow the shame in his voice as he whispered. "This is your child."

Kneeling before her, Sala gently cupped Zosia's cheeks. The white blonde hair was gone. The chubby rosy cheeks had also disappeared. In their place were boils and sores. The men had wanted Zosia to learn how to be quiet, and now Sala wondered if she would ever speak again. Only in the shape and color of her eyes could Sala find the child she had left. "Oh, my Zosia ... what have I done to you?"

"Mamusia."

One word, filled with all the love and forgiveness only a child could grant. She folded Zosia in her arms and sobbed into her stubbly head. These monsters had almost killed her girl, all because she had let her go.

She would never make such a mistake again.

When she rose, Zosia was still wrapped in her arms. It no longer mattered to her what the men said, she would never leave a child of hers again. For the first time since they viewed the massacre, the image of the destroyed little girl with half of her face missing started to fade away.

In the meantime Antony had disappeared, and when he joined her again, she couldn't help but ask, "Where did you go?"

"I thought I would make sure to get Zosia some reparation for their abuse."

"What do you mean?"

Antony held out a bag filled with potatoes. "These will help you put some meat on her bones."

She did not know what else to say. At that moment she realized Manek was standing close by her side. He had been so quiet she had almost forgotten he was there. She looked down at him and took his hand. They were together again, from here on out. They would live together, or they would die together. No exceptions.

CHAPTER NINETEEN

Thank goodness for the Dziedics. After Antony returned the hollow shell of what had once been her lively daughter, they went directly to their neighbors. Winter was coming, and shelter from the cold had to be found. She had no desire to go back to the woods, back to those men she no longer trusted would look out for them. The Dziedics would help them until she found shelter for the winter, they always did. And in the meantime, hiding in the attic of the barn, with her two children beside her, under the hay, would be a welcome relief to the months of agony she had endured without her child.

Zosia had endured too much. Straightaway, Sala set out to help Zosia heal from the trauma of her abandonment, both body and soul. Her child's hair and body began to fill out again, but no longer would her daughter yell or make much noise at all. All those months she had been living with the hens, told to "guard the chickens." Sala could only pray that her daughter would one day forget this nightmare and never look back.

It was November and an early snowfall fell upon Brzostek. Sala knew this was not a good sign of the winter to come. To make things even worse, Zosia became ill with the measles. The fever she suffered was terrifying in their primitive conditions. Sala would go out to get snow and ice and try to pack her small, fragile child until the fever finally broke. The constant guilt that she had led her poor baby to death's door, and then the agonizing fear that she herself or Manek would also get sick, weighed heavy on her heart.

Finally, Zosia started to get better, and Sala decided she had to find more permanent shelter. She could not stay there for long. She had meant all along for the Dziedics house to be merely a temporary shelter. They had to keep moving. Not after that close encounter with the SS the time before. She could not afford any more holes in her coat.

Antony had not come around lately. She understood, but it did not help the feeling that everybody had abandoned them.

Instead she went out on her own. From house to house, she searched for someone willing to risk their lives to protect a Jewish family. With the death of her cousins Bunek and Isaac, she was sure she, the children and Ignash were all that was left of the Schonwetters. Most of the people she entreated were happy to take them. This eagerness scared her. No sane person would want to risk the wrath of the Germans. Sala suspected their open arms meant they saw an opportunity to profit from their presence. She knew they would turn her and the children in at their first opportunity, for nothing more than a jar of marmalade or a kilo of sugar. So she would move on.

Then she came to the Ribbas. From the rumors that the men brought back from their excursions during the summer, she had learned that he had hidden Jews in the past winters. He lived far from the Dziedics, so it alleviated the fear of Germans looking for her so close to her former home.

"Please take my children," she begged the farmer. "Hide us. Just for the winter. Come spring, we'll return to the forest and you'll never see us again."

"I can't. The Germans—"

Sala looked around at the farm in desperation. It was small, but it was well tended. They understood the rules Israel had taught her. The fields were tilled, and the one cow and herd of pigs were fat. "I beg of you. Please take us. I promise, I will give you a jewel if you do. Just for the winter, during the cold."

Mr. Ribba's piercing eyes were hooded with reluctance. "There won't be much room …"

"We won't mind. I understand farmers. We don't need much room. Hardly any at all. Just someplace warm during the winter and some food once a day. Please. I beg you."

"Fine. Fine. Come back tomorrow and I may have an idea."

She pretended to go, but she lingered in the forest to watch what the farmer did next. There were no German patrols nearby, and Mr. Ribba did not go to seek out the Kapos in the village. He remained busy in the stable for a long time, but other than that she saw no sign that he was planning to break his word.

Traveling as she did only at night, she made her way back to her children.

They started the long walk to the Ribba farm. Zosia did her best to keep up, but Sala's longer legs and Manek's quick pace meant she kept falling behind. Finally, Sala picked up her daughter to carry her. The sky grew dark fast, heavy clouds covering the moon, and the temperature dropped even faster. The snow on the ground only made the trek worse. Sala felt the cold seeping into her bones. Each breath was as if icicles were forming in her lungs, and her breathing grew slower from the effort.

It was just so cold. All she could do was keep moving, her arms tight around Zosia, who mercifully had fallen asleep. Their coats were so thin, the wind seemed to slice through them with no effort. Her hands were buried in her sleeves beneath her child, and she warned Manek to keep his inside his coat pockets.

Amid her fatigue a memory from long ago crept into her thoughts. The Jewish High Holiday, Rosh Hashana. The Jewish New Year, the holiest day. The house was warm as toast from all the baking, and fires blazed in every hearth. She could almost smell the challah as she walked, hear Manek laughing with David and Zosia as they played around the house, Manek helping with the...

Manek . . .

Sala whirled around as she suddenly realized she hadn't seen her son in a while. Running back through the snow, she found him face down in a snow bank, fast asleep. When she turned him over, she saw he had urinated on himself.

"Mamusia," Manek murmured, rubbing his eyes sleepily. "Give me a few more minutes, Mamusia. I will go and feed the dogs later."

He thought they were still at home.

"Manek," Sala said firmly, ruthless with fear. "You must wake up now."

"I can't, Mamusia."

"Yes, my son, you can. You can do anything. Look at how much you have already done. We must go. We must keep moving. You can do it, Manek. I would carry you if I can, but please, my son, please try to keep walking."

He sat up and rubbed his eyes. Then he looked down at his lap with horror and jumped out of the snow. "Mamusia ... I ... I ..."

Sala couldn't believe that even during this dark night she could find some humor in the situation. "Well," she gave him a smile. "At least half of you is warm."

"But, Mamusia, I ..."

"I know, don't worry. I won't tell if you don't."

Trying to hide the tears that threatened to fall, he finally smiled sheepishly. "Who would I tell, Mamusia?"

"Let's go to the Ribbas. Perhaps they'll have a warm room for us to sit in. We will worry about your clothing later."

At long last they finally approached the farmstead. It was so quiet, she feared it was deserted. Then she saw the puffing smoke streaming from the chimney. Sala brought the children to the stable and then used the flagstones to the house, to avoid leaving any footsteps in the sodden ground. Tapping on the window, she got Mr. Ribba's attention. He gave her a nod and motioned for her to wait.

When he came out of the house, she and the children followed him into the stable. He pushed aside a patch of hay strewn on the floor and wrenched up a hatch made from wood to reveal a ... grave.

"Get in."

"Excuse me?"

"Get in," he said.

Sala looked at Manek and back at her host, trying to process what he was asking of her. "You want us to get into a grave?"

"It is your hiding place."

"Is this what you were doing when you asked me to come back in a day?"

"Yes, digging this." He gestured again to the hole.

"I'm not getting into a grave," she said.

"Mamusia." Sala looked down with surprise to see Manek helping Zosia climb down into the pit. Ribba had only dug four feet down, but Manek was still careful to help lower his little sister into the hole without hurting herself. "Mamusia, look," he gestured at the low chopped-out walls. "It's warm. Nice and warm. We don't have to worry about someone seeing us through the trees, and the wind cannot reach us down here. We will be able to sleep, really sleep, and not have to worry about anything."

She was still reluctant as the farmer said to her:

"Listen, Mrs. Schonwetter, my wife and I go to church every Sunday. You can get out on that day as long as you stay inside the stable. I'll come by as often as I can with food and water for you all."

"How will you feed us?" Stepping into the pit felt like accepting a living death.

"There's a hole in the hatch," he showed her. "I'll use that."

She slowly lowered herself into the hole, watching her excited children. They were … happy? Happy to be buried alive?

"Mamusia, you sleep on that side, and I'll stay here. This way Zosia can be in the middle and stay warmest. It will be nice, Zosia. So toasty."

The three of them lowered their bodies to the ground. As Mr. Ribba slid the hatch over them, Sala found herself desperately seeking comfort. Then she felt it: Zosia's fingers, so tiny and frail, slid into her palm, instantly quelling her panic. Manek turned on his side and put his arm over Zosia so he could lay his palm on Sala's stomach.

Her children. They were reaching out to her.

They would stay together.

One heartbeat.

Two heartbeats.

They would be fine. All that mattered was they had each other. This time when her eyes closed, she felt herself drifting off to sleep and let the last of her concerns go.

CHAPTER TWENTY

How she dreamed. Once, Sala was the wife of the wealthiest farmer in the village. A man whose family went back generations as prosperous landowners. People came from all around for Israel's blessing. Her house was pristine, scrubbed daily. Her kitchen constantly filled with delicious food cooking, her apple cake cooling on the sideboard, making the house smell like a piece of heaven. But dreams had a way of turning into nightmares. Beautiful violets beneath her feet had slowly turned into broken attic floor boards that morphed into the floor of a grave beneath her. What happens, she wondered, when you cannot wake up from your nightmare? It becomes your reality.

The first morning when Manek asked how they were to go to the bathroom, Sala realized just how squalid living inside this hole would be. She directed him to turn onto his side and pee against the side of the pit. She and Zosia were not as fortunate in the way they were created. They were forced to just go where they lay. Ribba's hole gave them little room to move around; they could not even sit up. The first Sunday when they got out of the pit, she never wanted to run out into a snow bank so badly to reduce the unsanitary aspects of their new life on her clothing. Who would think that she would thank God that they were housed in a stable? At least, she told herself ruefully, the stench blended in.

She no longer dreamed of her nice home or longed for her husband's embrace. She closed her eyes and imagined the hottest, longest bath of her life. The water would be changed every few minutes with steaming hot water.

Her reverie was interrupted by Zosia's eager cry:

"What happened next, Manek?"

"The dragon rose on the wind and breathed fire over all of the Germans until they were crispy flakes, like coal in the fire. Their fiery breath came so hot, it melted the machine guns into pools of shiny metal."

"And then?"

"The dragons ate the Germans. They went crack and pop as the dragons gobbled them all down."

Zosia's laughter lifted everyone's spirits.

They wiled away the hours trapped inside in two ways. Either Sala would teach them their letters and numbers. Or they would tell each other stories. Miraculously, stuck inside this pit of dirt, her kids used their imagination to build entire fantasy worlds. They launched on grand adventures filled with exciting chases and interesting lessons. Usually they included the Germans meeting a horrible death.

Their only daily reprieve was when Mr. Ribba came with their rations. Some bread, some water, and on special days, they even got soup. He would brush aside the hay and lift a piece of wood to give them their food. Sala would either hold their heads up slightly so they could swallow, or they would try to angle on their side, propping slightly up on their elbows, to eat. Afterward, Mr. Ribba would ever so carefully replace everything back to the way it was, so it did not look like anything out of the ordinary had been disturbed.

After weeks of living inside their claustrophobic hole, the noise of approaching horses made all three of them go deathly quiet. "What is that?"

"Soldiers," Sala whispered, frozen with fear.

They fell silent, barely breathing. The horses' hooves stepped right over their heads, it felt like, and a German patrol started talking in the guttural language they barely understood. When after a time they heard the voices fade, she saw Ribba and his piercing eyes looking down at her through the hole. "The German soldiers are stabling the horses here for a few days while they search for you in the woods. Stay inside and keep quiet, all of you."

Having the Germans so close meant they not only had to stay quiet, but Ribba's actions were under constant scrutiny. He still brought them water, though, masking his movements because he had to water the animals. He had one cow, a small herd of pigs and now the two horses ridden by the Germans. The stable was packed. What the soldiers didn't realize was not only was their prey hiding beneath their feet, but by bringing in the horses, they increased the heat inside the stable. The Schonwetters were forced to take their coats off to cool down, though Sala warned the children to not get used to it.

She continued their daily routine, starting with their alphabet. Keeping one ear focused for sounds coming from above, listening for returning footsteps, she would have the children alternate reciting their letters in a whisper. Then she had them do the same with their numbers, forcing them to count as high as they could go. There was barely any light, save a small beam that was cast through a crack in the floorboard, so next she would make the numbers and letters with her fingers, drawing an invisible character on their forearms and quiz her children. Their bodies might atrophy from being stuck in a prone position for so long, but their minds would continue to be nimble and quick. "What is four plus four?" She quietly whispered. Each of them would make the answer using their fingers. Sala would feel for their answers, smiling when they both got it right. These types of games not only taught them, ate up their waking hours, but also was a way for them to feel they were playing while still keeping quiet.

Her ears were constantly straining to hear the soldiers return.

No matter how she felt about how things had turned out in the forest, she hoped they did not find Fish, Ignash and Romek. Before she left, not realizing she would not return but perhaps anticipating it, she had warned them not to leave their hiding place until the farmers started to plant, but the chances they would listen to her seemed slim.

When the Germans finally left, they let out an enormous sigh of relief. "What do you think it means, Mamusia?"

"The front is getting closer and the Germans more desperate."

"This is good?"

Sala smiled at her two curious children. "This is very good, my loves."

They could hear the sound of soldiers on the wind sometimes. Sala had learned this had become a war of nations. The German voices made them shake with fear. But the Russian ones gave her and the children hope. If the Russians were beating the Germans back, perhaps the war would not continue forever. Perhaps, please God, perhaps they would get to live again. The Germans hated the Russians almost as much as the Jews. Surely if the Russian voices were growing closer it was a good thing?

Farmer Ribba, however, had been spooked. He came to them a few days later in the middle of the night and ushered them out of the hole. Sala was petrified that he was going to tell them to leave. Winters were harsh in the Jaworze Forest. "What is the matter?" she whispered.

"We cannot take a chance that they will come back. I have dug another hole. Come with me."

Ribba walked out of the barn and across to the pigsty. To her disgust, Sala saw that right under the "house" for the pigs was another hole that Ribba had dug for her and the children. She could tell he must have been digging a little each night and then trying to spread the dirt all around, to keep from drawing attention to what he was doing.

"A stable they might think to look for hidden Jews, but a pigsty, no one would ever think, or even want to walk over here. You will be safer."

Sala could not argue with that thinking, but the thought of living beneath the pigs turned her stomach. She ushered the children down and into the hole. Just before Ribba placed a wooden slat over the opening, he turned to them.

"I will come back when you can come out into the pen to stretch your legs. I will take the pig out and only bring it back if the Germans are near. But stay hidden just in case. I will be back with some bread and water tomorrow."

He then left as quickly as he came, and Sala pulled the children close. Their plight had come to this: she was now beneath the one animal that she grew up not only avoiding, but that was also the symbol of loathing in the Jewish religion. How appropriate, she thought.

That Sunday, while most of the town went to church, Ribba returned and let them out into the pen. They only had a short time to stretch until the parishioners finished their service and started to make their way back to their homes. They huddled in the pen. Manek did as he always did: he looked out through the slits in the fence at the world outside with a dreamy look in his eyes, along with a sadness that broke her heart.

Zosia went to kneel next to him. "Manek, after this war is over, I am going to get you something special to eat. No one really knows about it. It is dark, and sweet, and melts in your mouth. It is called 'chocolate'!"

"Oh please, nothing like that exists. It is just another one of your fairy tales, but I must say, you have a huge imagination!"

"No, it does, it does, I promise!"

"Let me tell you, little sister, what we are going to do after this war is over. I am going to let you fly! We are going to go on a machine called a plane! It flies in the air, and we will be able to go anywhere you want!"

Zosia, already upset that her brother did not believe her story, rolled her eyes. "Oh I do not believe you! There is no such thing as that. Stop lying. That would be too heavy, and you would need a rope to hold it up. Now who has the huge imagination?"

Sala chuckled to herself listening to her children's banter. She silently prayed that one day they would each live out the other's dreams.

$$* * *$$

It was quite some time until they were let out again. More German army units kept appearing in the area, and each time Ribba feared they were nearby, he would put the pig back in the pen above them. No one would ever look under a pig. Yet at the same time the conditions in their grave became almost unbearable. The boards above them that hid the opening of their hole had slits that could not hold out the excrement and urine that would come free flowing from the pig. They were rained upon with the pig's waste, and there was nothing they could do but turn as much as one could to try to avoid it entering their mouth or nose.

She wiled the days away with their usual games. Zosia and Manek would use her fingers as dolls. Just feeling their tiny hands within her own palm would give her the strength and resolve to carry on. She would try to make up the wildest stories, and in each the pig became just as big of a villain as the Germans, with both their fates destined for destruction. Although she was so proud of her children for their endurance, she was heartbroken that their experiences were so demeaning and stunted.

When Ribba finally came one day at dusk to let them out, she thought she would cry with relief. She didn't realize until she got out that it wasn't just the pig that had heated up the pit; the weather had turned. Poland was emerging from its icy grip.

"Mamusia?" Manek called, sitting by the door of the sty staring out at the livestock. He and Zosia had been whispering while looking out through the small holes, as they always did. "Why is it the chickens can run free and we cannot? Why are we less than the chickens?"

"Yes, Mamusia. Why?"

"All these animals, they can look for food when they want, they can play when they want, and they can run around when they want. We are so much bigger than those little birds, but we have to stay here."

Sala knelt before her children and hugged them tight to her chest. "One day," she promised. She put a hand on each of their shoulders so she could look them both directly in the eye. "One day, I swear, you shall run as free as the chickens and be as wild as the wind. You will climb trees, and race with your friends through the trees, and walk in the sunshine, warm upon your faces. One day this war will be over, so be patient, my children. We will be happy once again."

"One day, Mamusia."

They were alerted by a commotion. Sala stood and rushed over to the door. *What was all that noise? What on earth?*

Then she found out why.

Three German soldiers rode into the farm as if they owned everything they saw. They were thick with glowing health, their uniforms pristine as their shining horses' coats. In comparison, she and the children were pale skeletons that would crumble in one good gust of wind. She saw the Ribba family running out their back doors in fear.

What should she do?

One heartbeat.

If they stay, they'd be found. If they were found, they'd be killed.

Two heartbeats.

What should she do? *Israel, what should I do?* His laughing visage filled her mind. *You, my Sala, will always run toward danger when the entire world would scamper away. The difference between you and fools is that when others would get burned by the fire, you will always find a way to tame the flame.*

Run toward the danger.

She silently asked her two children for forgiveness and then slapped each across their face. Grabbing each of their hands, she ran out of the pen. She knew she could not be found hiding in a pigsty. She ran right up to the soldiers before they could see where she was coming from and started screeching at them in Polish. "Did you see him? Did you see the monster? Have you seen what he did to us? Look at my children, they are wasting away. He will not feed us, he barely lets us out of the stable."

"Wait, wait, lady. Not so fast."

Sala turned to the soldier who seemed to understand her language and began her tirade from the beginning. She felt Zosia hiding her face in her skirts. Manek was trembling next to her leg so hard, she could feel it throughout her body. "You speak Polish?"

"I do, but you must speak slowly. What has happened here? Why are these children so malnourished? They are bone thin and filthy!"

"This pig of a man. We were in the next town, but when the fighting came and my husband died, we left. The man here told us that he would take us in, feed us. But he was cruel. They do not give us enough food to eat, he treats us as animals." She felt the bile rise in her throat as she spoke the unkind words.

Manek took off running.

"Come back!"

She chased after her son, and the soldiers followed her. Manek ran into the house and dove underneath the bed. Sala looked between the confused soldiers and her cowering child, quickly picking up her tale. "See what I mean? The monster who lives here beats us every day. This is why my son is so afraid. He thought you were coming to beat us as well."

"He really does not feed you? He has a cow for milk." He pointed the lone cow in the pasture.

"Never. The milk is not for us. The bastard," she spit out the word from her lips.

"This is not right."

When the soldier said those words softly to himself, she knew they would be fine. The German soldiers were not like the SS. Most of these men were conscripted into service, and they might not have any love for the Nazis at all. Kneeling on the floor, she reached under the bed to pull her son out. "Come, my child. These are good men. They are not like the monster who has held us prisoner for so long. They will not hurt you."

She heard the soldier translating the situation to the others. When he was done speaking, one of them gestured to Manek under the bed. He managed the one word "Come," which told Manek that he did not have to hide.

Outside, she saw they had thrown a rope on the cow and were preparing to take him.

The soldier gestured to a bench for her to sit with the two children. "You will wait here, lady. We will come back here with food for you and the children. When the man returns from wherever he's run, tell him he can come to our camp to get his precious cow back."

"What will you do?"

"Not your concern, lady. We will explain the proper way to treat future German citizens from now on."

Sala could not feel relief. She did not feel anything. This war had taken so much from her. She had nothing left to lose. Her family was gone, her dignity had been stripped away, and the ease with which she could lie stunned her. Survival had become an instinct she blindly obeyed.

The soldier who spoke Polish did return and brought them bread, cheese and even some jam. He told them that if they needed anything else, they were stationed nearby and she should come to them, because they would provide her and the children with more food. Who would have ever thought?

They ate it all outside, enjoying the fresh air. Sala let the children stay where they were, reluctant to force them back in the hole. Not until later in the evening did Mr. Ribba come creeping out of the woods. When he saw them all in his front yard, as bold as you please, he jumped with shock. "You're still here? I thought you all … I mean, we thought we heard gunshots."

"Gunshots? No. No gunshots."

Ribba went into the house, clearly checking what the Germans might have taken. Once he went to the stables, he found his crushing loss. He rushed over to her, his eyes bulging from his face.

"Where is my cow?"

"Your cow is with the Germans. They took it, but I would not try to get it back. Leave it be. I told them we were Polish refugees and you had given us refuge in your stable." No need to go into details, she thought.

She rose and gestured the children to her side. "We will not stay here any longer. They believed the story and we should be thankful, but not stupid. We will leave in the morning. You have been more than kind and generous."

She placed her hands on her children's shoulders and they walked into the stables.

"Tonight, my lovely children. Tonight we shall sleep on top of the hay rather than beneath it. And tomorrow we return to the woods."

Settling in, Sala sighed with ecstasy at feeling hay underneath her, the warmth of the children on either side of her, and the comfort of their bed. "This is much better than our usual bed of leaves or dirt, isn't it?" Zosia nodded sleepily, already drifting away. Looking at Manek, she couldn't help but ask him something that was bothering her. "Son, why did you run from the soldiers? It worked out fine in the end, but your Mamusia was handling it."

"I remember what I was once told."

"What?"

"Mamusia, you and Zosia can hide that we're Jewish. I cannot."

"Your coloring is the same as mine."

Manek's big, solemn eyes stared at her, waiting for his mother to realize what he meant. When she didn't guess, he looked down at his lap. "Poppa told me once, Mamusia. There is a way for men to always know if they are Jewish or not. I didn't wish the soldiers to do it."

"Do what?"

"Remove my pants."

"Why on earth did you think they would remove your pants?" Sala suddenly realized what was scaring her child. He was circumcised when he was seven days old. It had happened so long ago, and the ancient Jewish covenant was a matter of a ten-minute ceremony. How smart her child had become. "I see. I understand, Manek."

"You understand now?"

"I do, Manek. I apologize for not thinking about it sooner."

"Why would you, Mamusia? It's not like you have one."

The two of them giggled at his silliness. "I will not forget again," she promised.

"Mamusia ..."

"Yes, Manek?"

"Could we please have a treat when we go to the forest?"

"What would you like?" Sala wondered what a normal ten-year-old would want. Manek hadn't asked her for anything in four years. What did he miss? What did he long for? A toy? An adventure? A special type of food? "Tell me, my brave boy. What would Manek like most of all?"

"A bath," he answered. The stables rang out with their laughter.

CHAPTER TWENTY-ONE

In the forest, the first thing she did was deliver on the much needed bath. A stream didn't provide the immersion-in-hot-water dream she'd been having for weeks, but that was the only option she had. She took a pail from the Ribbas and some soap. Their clothing was little more than rags at this point, but they became officially clean, or as clean as she could manage. The soap didn't last longer than the second child's bath, but at least her children were glowing again. Yet a drawback was that once their skeletal bodies were no longer hidden by mud and grime, their bones seemed to protrude out even farther.

The quiet in the forest had disappeared. The roads that ran through their neck of the woods were now filled with an exodus of people escaping the front, which was getting closer. Even though they were not as gaunt as she and the children, the look of despair was familiar. They at least had left with as many belongings as they could carry, either on their back, or in baskets that they held.

She also kept seeing groups of armed men. One, Army Ludowa, the People's Army, were not so bad. None of them held anti-Semitic views. However, another group was a different story. The Home Army, Army Krajowa, was a lawless bunch who were said to be as violent and filled with hate against the Jews as the Germans were. The problem was, it was impossible for Sala to tell them apart.

Hunger was the most pressing problem, though. She was appalled at how thin all three of them had become. They returned to their "home" from last summer, the prearranged meeting place she and the men had discussed. Yet they found little to eat. Day after day their three former companions did not appear, and the mushrooms were gone. She knew she had to do something. Starvation would kill them before the Germans. So one morning, she left Manek in charge of Zosia and went out to explore. Stopping at the nearest village, Sala was shocked at how devastated it was. Signs of fighting appeared on the houses. The war had finally come to surround them.

The retreat of the German army not only brought more danger. Its soldiers ate food faster than hungry children.

So she did the one thing she swore once to never do.

Returning to the clearing later, Sala could hear Manek softly telling Zosia another of his exciting adventure stories. So like a boy. Even with the violence and terror surrounding them, he still loved to tell tales of mighty heroes accomplishing great deeds. She wished she had some whimsy still inside her soul so she could share a story with them as well. They asked, but she had no thrilling, courageous tale. No memory of daring escapades from the past to stave off their boredom. She had only fears for their future.

"Come, my wonderful children. I have a surprise for you."

"What is it, Mamusia?"

She sat down at the fire they'd made and began to empty her pockets. Her soul might be empty, but she knew how to make a meal fun. It was the gift of every good Mamusia. "I found a secret treasure." She bumped Zosia's shoulder with her own. "Guess what is inside?"

"Is it gold?" Zosia asked.

"Blankets and pillows?"

"Much better." First she pulled out a pan and set it on the hot coals. Next, from the depths of her coat, she pulled the burlap sack, half-filled with flour.

"Are you going to make bread? Out here?"

"No, Manek. This is impossible for even your Mamusia."

For her next move, with a dramatic flourish, Sala pulled out the cloth covered package she had been both repulsed and joyful to find. Opening it up, she showed it to the children, who looked at it with confusion. "This is a magical substance you have never had before. It is only to help us tide over our tummies until the men return and help find food."

"What is it, Mamusia? What is it called?"

"It is ... bacon!"

The two children made appropriate oohing noises. Sala chopped up the cured pork and put it in the hot pan. Once some grease coated the bottom of the pan, she mixed in the flour, using the knife to help her combine the two ingredients. The results were an oddly colored type of cake, but it was the best they could do. At least the children would have meat and something hot and filling for them.

Cutting it with the knife, she used clean leaves to wrap pieces so the children could eat without burning their fingers. Manek, the hardest critic of all, was the first one to bite into it. His eyes closed, and he made a mmmm noise which seemed to indicate it was safe. Zosia didn't wait for long. As soon as she saw Manek liked it, she started to eagerly gobble hers up.

"Mamusia?"

"Yes, Manek."

"If this war ever ends, I hope you make this for us every day. This is the best food I have ever tasted in my whole life."

They all giggled at his joy. As her children broke one of the firmest rules of being a Jew, she silently sent an apology to her husband for this crime. Starving to death would surely insult the Lord far more than two little kids eating pork, she pointed out to him. Keeping Kosher was something all Jews did, but few Jews went without food for so long. Fewer still were watching their children waste away before their eyes. When there was one piece left, Zosia and Manek both insisted she eat as well. She tried to hide how much she liked it, but they quickly saw through her expression. "Maybe you were right, Manek."

"Every day, Mamusia. That was delicious."

A few days later the three men finally appeared.

She and the children were so excited to see Fish, Ignash and Romek. All their disagreements from the summer before were forgotten. Yet she had to raise the problem she'd been trying to keep from the little ones. The weather had been long and hard on the land. They'd barely found any food the few short days they were here. The forest would not be the haven she'd come to expect. She explained all this to her cousin.

"We have a surprise for you three."

Sala turned when she heard Ignash talking. "What have you three done?"

Romek went to a stump in the center of their favorite clearing and brushed away the dead leaves. He'd buried a trunk halfway in the dirt so that only the lid could be accessed. "On my way here, I saw a big truck. The two German soldiers got out to go and ..." he glanced at Sala and Zosia, "relieve themselves. While they were busy in the bushes, I snuck up behind them, pulled the knife I have, and cut their throats. After they were dispatched ..." At Sala's horrified expression he shrugged. "Two less Germans has to be a good thing. Well, after they were taken care of, I got busy in the back of the truck. Much to my surprise, it had just what we need." With an exaggerated flair Romek and Fish opened the trunk to reveal ...

"Food," the three Schonwetters yelled in unison.

Crackers, biscuits, jam, canned meat, even cheese. Forgetting the means by which Romek had "procured" the food, Sala wiped her eyes with the relief of seeing so many choices. It had been years since their diets had any form of variety. She wasn't sure if she even knew how to eat so many different things at once. Her stomach might die from shock.

"This is ..."

Ignash pulled her into his embrace, hiding her tearing eyes against his coat. "We know, Sala. We can eat for a few weeks from this alone."

"We have more," Fish told the children.

He and Romek next uncovered another stash, this time of weapons. "We will use these to protect our women," Romek said. "Manek, you must learn how to shoot them so when we go on raids to find supplies, you will feel safe."

"The women will feel safe," Manek corrected him.

Sala wondered if she'd ever feel safe again. They could have stolen an entire factory of weapons and she would still be scared. There were Germans, Kapos, Volksdeutche, militias which were impossible to tell apart, and Polish collaborators willing to trade the lives of Jews in for a crust of bread.

"What will you take next?" Sala asked.

Ignash looked at their clothes and smiled. "I think it is time we found you three something else to wear."

Sala laughed as the children cheered. *Perhaps it would be okay.*

The next day, they started to train Manek on how to use the gun. The rifle looked like an instrument of evil to Sala, but her child regarded it as a longed-for step toward adulthood. He was ten years old, about to be eleven. If the war hadn't happened, he'd be an experienced helper in the fields, walking in the footsteps of his father, as Israel had done so in his. Her son would be used to going to shul, driving the wagon by himself, even attending Israel's meetings with town leaders. He would have friends, and be thoroughly schooled in reading, writing, mathematics, history, science and of course, being a good Jew. They had money once. He would know birthday presents. He would have a bath every day, his clothes washed each week.

Instead he was sitting in the dirt, meticulously taking apart a rifle, cleaning it, and putting it back together again.

She refused to touch the weapon, a decision the men agreed with, yet Sala remained uneasy. Being armed did not help their main problem. They had food from Romek's raid on the supply truck, but they were going farther and farther each night to find them more supplies. The forest was frighteningly bare. The nearest farms were idle, the soil dry, the cattle skin and bones. On the roads all they saw were people, refugees, looking for food just as much as they were. Sala didn't like the snippets of conversations she was able to catch from the stream of tired women and haunted men. Worst was the endless despair written into their children's faces. The towns all around them had no food. The cities were deserted. Villages still had limited supplies, but the earth had turned its back on the Polish people.

Just as the world had turned away from the plight of the Jews.

When the area was clear of people, Ignash and Fish would help Manek with his shooting. They would have him practice on leaves and small branches on the trees for targets, cautioning the boy to never take a shot unless he was positive he was going to hit what he aimed for.

Rifles were easy to find. Bullets were far more rare.

"Come on, it will be funny."

"What?"

"You'll see," Fish told Romek.

The next day, Romek and Ignash went to the next village to visit their new sweethearts. Sala saw Fish sneaking away from the camp when she returned from the stream with a fresh bucket of water. She didn't think anything about it. Zosia was sorting tea leaves for her, and Manek retrieved some crackers and jam from the stash when he whirled around and stared at a group of bushes with suspicion.

Manek ran to the rifle, loaded it, and calmly aimed at the rustling foliage.

"What's wrong?"

"Someone is coming," Manek said. "I'm going to protect you."

"Put down the weapon, Manek."

"I am sorry, Mamusia, but I cannot. I hear someone coming."

"Manek, please."

"I must protect you and Zosia, Mamusia."

"Manek, put down the gun." Sala yelled as loud as she could.

Fish took that moment to jump out of the bushes, laughing his fool head off. "I almost got you, Manek." He chortled. "You should see your faces. Manek, you are white as a cloud. Your Mamusia's voice was so loud she probably brought the entire army down on our heads."

He held his sides as he continued to laugh at his great joke. Sala saw Manek un-cock the gun and, with shaking hands, place it back against the tree where he had snatched it. "You idiot," Sala yelled, whacking Fish in the back of the head over and over. "He was ready to shoot you. With all of the dangers we are facing, why would you invite such pointless tragedy? How could you do such a thing? Have you no sense? No sense at all?"

"Sala … Sala … It is fine." He kept laughing as he held his hands over his head where she was hitting him, trying to protect himself.

"If my son had to live with killing a friend of his, I'd dig you up from your grave just to shoot you again!" Sala continued to hit the fool, her temper red-hot, her patience burned through. The idea her son would have to live with such a crime, after all the other horrors of his childhood, made her want to scream at the injustice to the heavens. Instead, all she could do was hit the laughing man until her arms were tired. After a while, she continued just because it was making Manek and Zosia laugh as well, and that sound was worth any effort.

When she sat down once more, her heavy breathing was the only sound in the clearing. Fish came to her on a bent knee to offer her a cup of water and a cracker with cheese. She took them begrudgingly.

"Manek," he said. "Make sure you marry a woman like your Mamusia one day. I cannot think of a wiser choice a man can make than to have such a woman by his side."

Her son's eyes, so large and solemn, took in Fish's face, turned to Sala and nodded.

Spring turned to summer, and still no wild edible food appeared. The men were getting more daring with their "expeditions." Sala knew the long forays would catch up to them eventually. What concerned her the most was the coming cold. It had been hard enough to find a place to stay during the winter last year, and she suspected this time it would be impossible. She had thought that perhaps she would try to go back to Ribba, beg him again to take them in. Living with a pig was horrible, but being turned in or caught was far worse.

One day, while hearing the men talk about the latest news they had heard from the outside world, she caught them mention Ribba's name.

"Ignash, what did you say about Ribba? What happened?"

The men exchanged sideway glances. They knew she had gotten shelter at the Ribba farm the winter before.

"I don't think you will be going back to him for shelter anymore," Fish replied, lowering his head.

"Why, what has happened?"

None of the men spoke at first. Finally, Romek looked at her solemnly. "They are all dead."

Sala gasped, it could not be. With barely a whisper, she dared to ask, "How?"

She knew the answer before he spoke.

"Those filthy Germans heard they were Jewish sympathizers. They said they found out they were hiding Jews. They took the children first. Made the parents watch as they executed them right in front of them. And then they turned their guns on them. Left them to rot, right there, right in front of the stables."

She could not afford to be consumed with guilt, or despair, or grief. She had to close off every part of herself that wanted to feel. She had thought she had hit rock bottom before, but it seemed now that the pit was a bottomless well. She had suffered enough deprivation, but she had nowhere to turn. And worst of all, her next thought was, now where will I go?

The constant stress of what to do, where to go, how bad could it actually get, was horrible. She could feel that something even worse was yet to come. And happen it did, but not until the summer was fading, and unfortunately, when it did, it was far worse than she could imagine.

Romek and Fish came running into the camp one morning at dawn. Sala exclaimed when she saw their panicked faces and the blood on their upper bodies, "What happened?" She went to feel their chests to see where they were hurt, and that's when she realized what was missing.

Ignash was gone.

"The police," Fish said.

"The bastards are trigger happy." Romek knelt at the bucket and tried to wash his hands. Fish kept himself busy getting out fresh clothes for them to change into. "The police were in the village we targeted. We haven't raided that place in a while, but still we went back too early. The bastards were there."

"Is Ignash alive?" *Silly, Sala. Of course he wasn't.* If he was alive, he would be here. *So is Israel dead?* As always, when she asked that question, she made herself stop looking for an answer. *He isn't here.* This was all she could be sure of. But Ignash, her cousin, also wasn't here. The blood covering these men's chests didn't portend a good outcome for him. She breathed a sigh of relief when she saw Manek was still asleep. Zosia would only wake if Manek shook her.

"We ran as fast as we could."

"But they were shooting at us," Fish said.

"And Ignash was hit?"

Fish and Romek shared a look that made her uncomfortable. *What happened to her cousin? What did they do?* "Yes," Romek said. "Ignash was wounded by the police. We tried to help him. We carried him for what felt like miles. But, in the end, he was struck by another bullet."

"We tried, Sala." Fish said. "We tried to carry him. He was so heavy and the police were getting closer."

She kept looking between the two of them. She saw the guilt in their expressions for not bringing Ignash away safely. They could be feeling badly for other reasons, she realized. But deep inside her gut, she didn't think so. And now she had one more thing to fear.

"How far away did this happen?"

"Very far," Romek swiftly answered.

"This is why it took you so long to get back?"

"No," Fish said. "We made sure to go in a roundabout path so the police couldn't follow."

"Just in case," Romek assured her. "To keep you and the children safe."

"Right." Sala gave him a small smile as she hid her clenched hands in the folds of her skirt. "That was wise of you."

"Ignash would have wanted you to be safe."

"And you," she quickly told Romek. "Will one of you take watch?" Fish nodded. "Then I am going back to bed, gentlemen." Sala walked over to her sleeping children. She lay down next to Zosia, Manek on the far side. Just as she was going to close her eyes, she saw Manek's open. He nodded to her, then his eyes flickered downward. She followed his gaze and saw his hand was on his rifle, lying safely between him and his sister, covered by the ever present shawl. She let out a deep breath and nodded to him.

Her son. Her rock. He already knew what she was trying to accept.

The next day, they prepared to leave Romek and Fish behind.

CHAPTER TWENTY-TWO

So many groups of people straggled along the roads, it would be easy to pick one to merge with. Sala tried to be smart. Fish and Romek warned her to keep their Jewishness a secret for as long as they could. Before they set out, Sala drilled the children on the new names they all had to adopt.

Each year at the high holidays, Jewish people repented for their sins in order to be deemed worthy by God, written in the Book of Life. Sala hoped that should God be watching, he write both their Jewish and their new pretend names down in that book, and not the Book of Death. It was especially ironic, for rather than going to shul to hear the blowing of the shofar, the ram's horn, they had only the thunderous explosions of the Germans' heavy artillery to herald their fresh year.

Sala wondered if any of the gaunt faces walking around had ever broken matzo or lit Friday night candles. Where were all the Jews? Was Manek right? Were they the only ones left? Almost a third of Brzostek was Jewish, and Israel once told her that almost ten percent of the entire population of Poland was Jewish. What did the Germans do with all those people? Surely they couldn't all be in mass graves and labor camps. The entire countryside would be nothing but an endless cemetery.

As she watched people passing from her hiding spot, she listened carefully for the names of the villages they hailed from. If she was to be responsible for their safety, she would need as much information as she could gather in order to pass as just another displaced person. She understood that knowledge would help keep them alive even more than food.

Sala, Manek and Zosia started out with one group, and when she saw another group behind her, she let the children lag until they left the first behind and joined with the others. She wanted to do this a few times, counting on the children's slower pace to mask the fact that they hadn't been moving with the refugees the whole time.

"Who are you?" asked an older woman, leading the pack she had just joined.

"I am Francizka; this is my son, Maryan; and my daughter, Zofia." Sala introduced them to the stranger. Her kids, as quick as they always were, gave the woman weary smiles.

"Where are you from?"

Resisting the urge to put the woman in her place for her inquisitive nature, Sala pasted a friendly smile on her face. She could not give in to frustration. She needed to act as "normal" as possible. She gave the woman the name of the farthest village she had heard from one of the other groups. They had been talking about how fierce the fighting was there.

"Oh. That's very far. No wonder you three are so skinny."

"The fighting was right near my house, so we had to leave."

Once they switched a half dozen times, Sala felt as if they had the routine down pat. She saw no hesitation in either child when she called them by their new names, and was thankful their old names were so easy to modernize. They didn't even notice that she had changed her name. To them, she was, and would always be, simply Mamusia. Just what every other Polish child called their mother.

It felt as if they walked for weeks. The winter was slow in coming, so sleeping on the side of the road was not so bad. But food? Finding something to eat was impossible. Empty fields were checked for a spare potato. If they were lucky enough to find one, the children were so hungry they were happy to eat it raw. Berries were gobbled straight from the bush; the entire time all three of them were scared one of the other refugee families would see the berries as well and they would have to share. Her two children, already emaciated beyond recognition, seemed to be wasting away right in front of her eyes.

Yet Maryan and Zofia never cried or complained once.

When Sala saw a home on the outskirts of a new village, filled with other refugees, she thought maybe they could rest for a while from their exodus. The woman who owned the house was rushing around helping people. Sala could tell the building was filled with others in need. "Please, please … can you take us in as well? I can see how many you are helping, I am just hoping you have space for three more, not really even three, just me and my two little kids."

"There's no space."

"I am begging you. We don't take up much room. We just need a place to stay for a little while to take a break from the walking."

"No."

"Please."

"There's nothing I can do."

"We just need some rest. I will go on my knees if you wish. You have so many people here, let me be your helper. I have two good working hands."

Finally, the woman relented. "All I've got left is the attic. You don't want to stay there, we have nothing else up there."

Sala resisted the urge to confess that an attic would be pure luxury to them at this point, especially after months stuck in a hole in the ground in the stables. Manek and Zosia were so exhausted, and she was scared they would get sick. Any illness at this point could kill them, because their bodies were so frail from lack of food and nonstop physical exertion. "The attic would be wonderful."

In they moved. Sala, Manek, and Zosia. All they had were their coats and her shawl to sleep on. The attic floor was made of boards that were smooth from age, so at least they didn't have to worry about splinters. They slept the first day away, luxuriating in the freedom of not having to worry about keeping moving with a group of people who were as defenseless and lost as they were.

The second day she started to hear the rumors as they went about their business. As she was collecting food from the countryside, helping cook for everyone, Sala began to hear a dangerous buzz. Most of it was directed at the woman who owned the home. *Who is she? Are you sure she's not Jewish? Look at all that dark hair and skin, she doesn't look Polish.*

Her family had lived, worked and died in this country for hundreds of years. She couldn't be more Polish if she tried.

Still, their tongues wagged, all about her and the children and their suspiciously dark features. *No husband? Something is suspicious there. What good Polish woman is walking through the country with no man?*

The owner's son was the worst of the bunch. That night, Sala caught the young man sneaking up the attic ladder. She had sent the children to bed on their own a few hours before. When Manek started screaming, she flew up the ladder. The young man was struggling with Manek, trying to pull his pants down. Her little boy wasn't giving in, though, holding onto his clothes and kicking out with all of his might.

She started yelling at the young man, accusing him of trying to violate her son. He was no more than a coward. Caught red-handed, he quickly disappeared back down the ladder.

After that she tried to keep the children close at all times. She wished she could leave, but where would she go?

The trouble was, they were children, and sooner than later, they escaped her supervision.

Sala had become aware that the men in the village brewed their homemade vodka at the house next door. She had seen their rudimentary work one day while taking out the garbage. They started with yeast-covered potatoes. Once that brew started to ferment, they would transfer it, to a large cauldron, cover it, and place it over a fire. Using a large stick through the hole of the cover, they mixed the mixture as it boiled to prevent any scorching. They had created some sort of pipe leading out of the mixture for the steam to escape, and the alcohol was captured in the glasses they lined up. She watched the men take turns stirring and tending to the pot, but as the German front got closer, the men started to get nervous. The approaching Germans, it seemed, did not appreciate what was seen as the Polish people's right. If they were caught, they would be shot and killed. So they hatched a plan.

They called Manek over one day to help them. The way they saw it, if the Germans did come upon their house and see their apparatus, all they would find is a kid making soup.

Manek did not know exactly what he was making, but he did know that it was important, and the men paid attention to him. He was eleven years old now, and he had a "job." These men lived in the same house as he did, they ate their meals together, and now they needed him. Being entrusted with the responsibility made him feel like a big shot.

Sala was fine with Manek stirring the barrel's contents and watching over the brew. They got extra potatoes, whether from the largesse of the men or when her son stole some extra from the crop. After a few days, when the brew was ready, they filtered it. She didn't realize they had reached that stage, or she would have kept Manek closer to her side.

* * *

"Come, Maryan."

Night was descending, and Manek had never been asked to join the men this late, so surely they needed him for something important. He really liked feeling this important.

"Remember the soup you have been stirring? It is called vodka. Do you know what that is?"

Not wanting to look like a child, Manek hesitantly nodded his head.

"Now we have to filter the liquid, to make sure no impurities are left. Come watch."

Another man pulled his hat off and started to use it as a strainer. A few others followed suit, and after an hour they had their vodka ready. They took their chairs and placed them in a circle.

"Come into the middle, Maryan." As he was ushered into the center of the seated drinkers, he was handed a small tin cup of their just finished vodka.

"Na zdrowie!" the first man toasted, raising his glass. "Thank you for working so hard to help us make our prize! Here is to Maryan!" As the first man swigged the liquor back, he motioned for Manek to do the same.

"Drink up, young man, you deserve it!"

Manek did not want to insult his new friends. He swallowed the clear liquid, and almost choked as it went down.

He had never tasted anything like it and hoped to never again. The back of his throat burned so badly, he was sure that he had torn a hole right through his neck. This horrible-tasting drink was something they had spent so much time making?

The man filled his glass again and gave him a wicked smile.

"Now it's your turn."

"What?"

"Don't be a child, be a man. I drank to your health. It is only proper that you now make a toast for my health and drink to me."

"I can't." Manek shook his head, trying to figure out how to escape the circle of men.

"Oh, don't worry, the first time is always the worst! You won't feel it soon, I promise. Take another drink."

And so he did. Before he knew what was happening, the next man in the circle stood up, refilled Manek's glass, and cheered again. "Na zdrowie, to Maryan!" and they all downed the vodka again as if it was water.

"Come, Maryan, your turn." And so it continued.

Soon Manek blearily looked at the men from his vodka-fueled haze. He had so many of the little glasses of clear liquid. What number was he on? Three? Four? He felt really good, though. Mamusia had never told him that vodka made you feel so good. The man was right. Sure, the first few shots burned like fire all the way down his throat. After that, though, he felt that fire warming him up from the inside. His tummy was full, and even his burps felt sweet.

For the first time since the war began, Manek was experiencing an unexpected bounty. There was so much vodka, and just he and five adult men to share it. He soon liked it, and every time the men refilled the little metal cup they gave him, he was just as happy as the others to slam it down.

"Na zdrowie!"

"Maryan, do you know any songs?"

"Of course I do."

"Sing us a song, little one!"

Manek knew plenty of songs. He opened his mouth and began to sing at the top of his lungs.

He could sing forever if they kept giving him vodka.

He was so absorbed with his singing, he barely noticed when one of the men approached him. Before he knew what was happening, the man started to unzip his pants. Manek did not know if he was singing or screaming at this point, but he did know he badly needed his Mamusia.

* * *

It was late, and Sala had no idea where Manek had wandered off to. As she started to search outside the house, she recognized her child's voice. Was that singing she heard? She crept up to the neighbor's house and peered into the window.

There he was, standing in the middle of the village men, drinking and singing. He barely registered the fact that the man behind him had an evil gleam in his eyes. Before she knew it, her child started to scream as the man reached for his pants zipper. Manek tried to push the adult man away, his breath coming in panicked gasps.

The terror Sala felt fueled a towering rage. She burst through the door breathing as much fire as a dragon in the stories Manek liked to tell Zosia. "You dirty old men," she bellowed. "Are you all queer? You try to rape my son? He is a little boy. You should all be ashamed of yourselves."

"Dirty Jew," one of the men hissed.

"We're just trying to prove what a liar you are."

"It isn't enough you try to rape my son. Now you insult me on top of everything else? I am going to the police and telling them everything you have been doing. Not to mention everything you tried to do to a little boy."

Sala grabbed Manek's hand and led him from the house, leaving the men with shocked expressions. They were much more afraid of losing their precious vodka than interested in proving she was a Jew. She helped Manek settle down in the attic, and she stayed up all night watching over them.

In the morning, even though he was so sick, she insisted they take off immediately. Manek was not sad to leave the house, and the strange men, far behind.

CHAPTER TWENTY-THREE

Sala could no longer keep track of the days or the direction they walked. She just knew they had to keep moving. The incident with the men turning on Manek constantly haunted her. Hiding the fact she was Jewish was clearly keeping them alive, but how long could she do that when it was emblazoned in the tint of their skin and the curl of their hair? Keeping them together meant everything to her, and she was terrified that should someone discover the truth, she would have no choice in the matter.

When they entered the village of Jaworze, she hoped the people might be more compassionate. The townsfolk lacked the antagonistic sneer she'd seen in so many faces. Hearing the hungry growls of her children's stomachs, she decided to try the one thing she hadn't so far. Going up to a couple standing outside a well-tended house, she took a deep breath. "I am so sorry to trouble you. My children are starving. Is it possible you have something, anything, you can share? They're so hungry, and we haven't been able to find anything to eat."

The couple looked at the two children, their cheeks hollowed out, eyes pits of need. "All we have is a boiled egg."

"We'll take it."

Sala almost swooned when the woman handed her an actual egg. She held it in the palm of her hand. "Thank you, thank you, thank you." Looking at her stunned children, she lifted her head, and rushed them a little way down the road. "Sit children." They sat on the curb and she carefully placed the egg in her handkerchief. Next she broke two small pieces from it, determined to keep the rest for the children to share later. Proving to her how desperately hungry they were, her children slowly savored their little pieces of egg, trying to make the sensation of eating last as long as possible.

Turning her head to keep the little ones from seeing the tears in her eyes, she caught the eyes of a woman in her early fifties walking by. Her long, straight blonde hair was caught in a brightly colored red shawl. Her eyes smiled as widely as her mouth. "Hello, you three. You look like you're enjoying a good meal."

"We aren't in your way, are we?"

"Of course not. I am Bronca, I live just down the street. Who are you?"

"I am Francizka, this is my son, Maryan; and my daughter, Zofia. We are from Brzostek. The war came to our village. We barely got out before the fighting came, so we couldn't bring anything other than the clothes on our backs."

"But where is your husband? Your family? Why are you traveling alone with two children?"

Sala couldn't stand telling another set of lies. Making up another story to save their lives. She was hungry and tired, too. When she looked up at the woman, she suspected all of the defeat she felt was reflected in her eyes.

Bronca took a deep breath, and Sala recognized the look of compassion in her eyes. She had seen that kind expression in others, like Antony and Heniek. "You know what? Why don't you and the kids come to my house and I will give you all something to eat."

It felt like a dream. Sala soon found herself seated at a table with Manek and Zosia, looking down at big bowls of borscht and potatoes. When she felt the tears coming from her eyes, she hid her face in her hands. Bronca squeezed her shoulder. "Eat, children. Your Mamusia will start in a minute."

After Bronca filled their bowls twice, and they had practically licked them clean, she had the children bed down on blankets in front of her fire while the two of them talked. Sala hoped whatever this woman wanted for her kindness would be a payment she could find it in herself to give.

"Do you have anywhere to go?"

"No. I thought if we kept ahead of the fighting ... but there's no food and the children are getting so frail."

"Okay, okay." Bronca patted her shoulder again and handed her a clean cloth to wipe her eyes. "My husband and I have plenty of room. Why don't you three take our spare room? You can sleep, eat, get fat again. We'll help you. It is the right thing to do. What do you think?"

"I couldn't impose."

"Nonsense, it will just be for a little bit."

Sala's emotions almost choked the words from her throat. But this kind woman was waiting for her to accept and she could not refuse. "Your gracious offer is beyond anything I ever imagined."

"My man will love having a boy around the house again."

"You are very kind."

"Not at all. I'm a wife and a mother myself."

"Which means?"

"I'm practical. More bodies in the house during the winter makes it easier to heat."

They laughed heartily until they saw they were bothering the children, so they hushed each other. Sala remembered a conversation like this she had with her husband once, and it made her feel at home.

Late that night, the children were unable to sleep from their long nap during the day, so she was able to softly explain what they would be doing while the rest of the house slumbered.

"But, Mamusia, how will we be like everyone else?"

"We will pretend," she told Zosia. "Don't you like having a warm place to sleep, food in your tummy and being clean, really clean, for the first time in years?"

"But how?" Manek asked.

"Follow the others. Do as they do. We must try, my children. These people are good to us, and we need the time to eat and rest. Our bodies are getting weaker from being on the move so much. Here we can recover."

Since the village was located on a major road, refugees began to stream through every day. Sala was thrilled that for once they had arrived first, so they already had a place to stay. Bronca took very few other people into her home, but she did her part, as the rest of the good-hearted folks did. Polish people were helping other Polish people against inconceivable odds of death, disease and starvation.

With all the activity came soldiers as well. Mostly they would drive through without stopping. Once, though, a jeep filled with men wearing uniforms with shining buttons pulled into the village center and stopped. Sala was outside playing with Zosia. When she felt one of the officers' eyes linger on her, she made an excuse and hustled her daughter inside. The man made her so nervous, she kept the children inside as much as she could after that.

That did not help the problem that arose in the next few days, however. Bronca kept casting worried looks her way, and she kept biting her lip as if there was something she wanted to say but was too kind to approach her. Finally, like water building behind a dam, Bronca broke, while they were taking a walk through the village square. "I must tell you something. Some people have started to talk about you and the kids. We are such a small village that three strangers are bound to stand out and cause loads of gossip. People say you all are not what you say you are."

"Not what we are?"

"They think you are a Jew."

Once again Sala recognized the only way to face this danger was to run full-speed towards it. "Who is it? Who is saying such things about us? Let me see if it is who I think it is." Sala's mind was moving faster than one of the German planes as it tried to decide how to respond.

Bronca was taken aback by her tone, but she pointed out the gossiper across the square.

"I knew it. I knew that is who you would say. I think she is the one who is a Jew. She says these horrible things about me and my family to divert suspicion away from her own self. I am going to go and tell her just what I think of her wicked ways."

"No, Francizka. No. Let me take care of it. Do not start any trouble now. We must remember who the true enemy is."

As Bronca went to talk with the woman, Sala tried to think if she had ever had any dealings with her. She had no idea who the woman saying the gossip was. She could only hope that somehow this would stop her from making any further trouble.

Lying to Bronca became a heavy weight on her soul. She also worried about how the children would cope if anything happened to her. Bronca and her husband were good to them, kind even. And Bronca's husband clearly liked having a little boy to go with him into the fields and work the land together. This was a safe place, and if she still believed, she knew it was an answer from God to her. Zosia loved Bronca and was content to spend hours in her kitchen making bread or peeling potatoes. It was a very safe haven indeed.

Finally, she decided that she could not deceive the woman any longer. "I must be truthful with you."

Bronca froze at her basin, dried her hands, and slowly turned to Sala. "What is it, Francizka?"

"We didn't know what to do anymore, or where to go. I just wished to protect the children. To be safe. You were so kind to us. I shouldn't have lied when we met. I should not have made it worse the other day when you asked me about the gossiper in the village."

"You are Jewish."

She flinched as if Bronca had struck her. It had been so long since she spoke the words out loud to someone else. Sala almost turned around to look at the door, convinced that some German officers would burst through and shoot her where she sat at the table. "I am."

"I suspected as much when we met."

"We'll leave in the morning."

"No," Bronca said. "No, don't do that. Stay with us, but don't tell anyone else what you have told me. I will keep you as a refugee, like all the others. Let's see how long we can get away with it."

"People are bound to talk again."

"You must watch what I do and copy me. Act like a Christian and the others will stop watching you. Tell your children each morning they should pray like everyone else. Each Sunday you will come to Church with us."

She had never considered such a notion. "We will try."

When she told the children that they had to go to church, she also told them that she was worried about how they would pass in a church, with everyone looking at them.

"Mamusia, I can teach you."

Sala looked at Zosia with a questioning glance.

"The family I stayed with last summer used to take me to church every Sunday. That was the only time I did not have to watch the chickens. I did what you taught us. I watched, I listened, and I learned. I can teach you and Manek what to do."

Sala had no words, she just smiled at her brave, smart child and hugged her. "Yes, we will learn from you. How about you start our lessons now?"

That Sunday, they went to church. Things went fine at first. At the end of the ceremony, the children even enjoyed eating the communion wafers. There was only one problem. Young Zosia had never had to do confession, and now Sala found herself on line with some of the other adults waiting to face the priest.

When it was her turn to approach the priest, Sala felt her heart beating hard enough to escape her chest. She entered the confessional and knelt before the robed man that sat on the other side of the wire window. She cast her eyes down, trying to decide what to do. She roughly understood the idea of this practice for the Roman Catholics, but she had no idea the proper way to do it. Thinking how much better she felt when she confessed the truth to Bronca, the sensation of again having someone on your side and not being so alone, she decided she would have to take a chance. There was goodness here. Surely that goodness extended to the church as well?

"Forgive me, Father. I do not know what to do. I am not a Catholic."

The priest looked up sharply, and Sala almost sobbed when the old man smiled at her and nodded a few times. She knew he had seen her many times in the village, and he seemed to like talking to Manek and Zosia.

He opened the barrier between them and placed his hand on her head to bless her. "You are a very brave woman. The war is getting closer to the end, and such a hero as you will survive."

Sala was shocked when he helped her rise. After the service he met her outside. He embraced her. "God will bless you, brave lady, and keep you and your children safe."

As she walked away, her eyes shiny with tears, the other women surrounded her with welcoming smiles. "Francizka, Francizka ..." Sala jumped when she realized they were talking to her. "You must not have any sins at all." Another added, "I've never seen the priest bless someone in person."

"What do you mean?"

Bronca smiled proudly at the other women in the village as she put her arm around Sala's shoulders. "The priest was so nice and cheerful when he spoke to you. He must really approve of such a devoted lady."

The other women all joined in the laughter, and Sala took the first deep breath she'd managed since they walked inside the village church. When she felt eyes on her, she found it was only Manek, checking that everything went well. She gave him a fast nod so he wouldn't worry and let herself be embraced by the female villagers.

The priest hadn't just blessed her in front of them. He'd given them an overt sign that she was one of them. She knew there would be no more gossiping talk about her little family. Between Bronca and the priest, she felt more secure than she had in years.

CHAPTER TWENTY-FOUR

The peaceful idyll would not last for long. Sala and Zosia were helping Bronca make borscht when the squeal of brakes cut through their idle talk. Sala looked at Bronca in terror, who shrugged. "Where is Manek?"

Bronca looked out the back window, "He must still be in the field with my husband."

The thunderous knocking made them grip each other in fear. "Open up."

Cleaning off their hands, Bronca went to the door. Sala sat down, pulling Zosia on her lap. In came two officers she'd never seen before, though judging by the lack of metal hardware on their chest, they couldn't be very high up in the German hierarchy. "Where is the lady with the two kids? The refugees you have living here?"

Holding Zosia's hand, Sala stood up, determined to not bring any trouble on these good people. "I am here."

The man looked down at his notes on his clipboard and scowled. "Don't you also have a son?"

"No, sir."

Bronca tried to stand up for her friends. "What is this about, officer? This is a good woman, the priest is very fond of her."

"He is not the only one."

"What?" Her hand tightened on Zosia's, who let out a small cry.

"You know our commanding officer, Hauptbefehlsleiter Muller."

"Why, yes, I have met him in the square on several occasions."

"He is at the hospital, and has asked that you come to him. He demanded I come and get you and your children, a boy and girl. If you have only a daughter, I guess I was mistaken. We must leave, though. He is quite ill and needs you by his side."

"No," she shook her head. "I can't leave."

"If you have no son ... why can't you leave?"

Her mouth opened and closed helplessly as her mind tried to come up with an answer. For once, she could not think fast in the face of danger. "Of course," she said. "You are right. If I must go, I must."

Bronca nodded slowly. "If you will excuse me."

"Go, go."

Sala watched with yearning as Bronca went out the back door, recognizing the woman was planning on hiding Manek. She turned back to the officer, who was giving another man instructions. "Let's go, lady."

The drive felt like it took hours. Zosia fell asleep, ensconced in her lap, her head on her shoulders. Her girl was nine years old, but given the lack of food for most of her life, her size was closer to a six-year-old. When they pulled up in front of the hospital, Sala was stuck in such a haze of fear and regret that she hadn't said goodbye to Manek that she didn't notice where they were at first.

"Go inside," the officer instructed her. "You are expected."

Sala and Zosia were taken to a room with a bed and some chairs. Lying there was the commanding officer from that day in the village square. At first he had just ogled her, but then he had spoken to her a few times. "You are here." His voice was reedy and thin, and he had a strange look in his eyes. Sala tried not to recoil from the heavy antiseptic smell. "This is good."

"What do you want from me?"

His eyes took her in slowly and her skin crawled in response. He licked his lips a few times and blinked his eyes. "Where is your boy?"

"I have only my daughter."

"Very well."

"Why am I here?" *You aren't Jewish, Francizka*, she reminded herself. *You are a good Roman Catholic woman. The priest promised you and the children would survive. You were blessed.*

"I am taking you to Germany with me. I will have you tend my house and work for my family."

"Oh. I ..."

When the man's eyes got a strange, detached look, she quickly shut her mouth. She didn't know what was going on here, but she knew when she was about to push someone too far. "You leave for Germany soon. I am having my aide arrange your passage now. Go to the room across the hall and wait for me there. I will let your child go with us since she is so beautiful."

She almost sobbed. *What was this man thinking to do with them?*

Feeling numb, Sala carried the still sleeping Zosia to the room across the hall.

A few minutes passed before a new officer walked past the open door. She managed to lift her ravaged face and look him in the eye. "Excuse me, fraulein. What do you think you are doing in here?"

"The officer across the hall said he has decided to send me to Germany to work for his family."

"What?" The man sighed and shook his head. He left without a word and she heard him stomp down the hall. When he returned, he was picking through a big ring of keys in his hand. "The man who called for you is not right in his mind. He is very sick, and the fever is causing delusions and ramblings. He may not even make it through the week. Go with your child. There is no need to come back here. I will make sure to tell the officers to not bother you again."

Sala nearly reeled in shock. The officer had to help pull her out of the chair. When they got to the back door, he used the key to open it.

As she stepped through the door he held open for her, Sala kept watching him fearfully as he closed the door. She turned back to the busy street, hoisted Zosia higher in her arms, and began to walk as quickly as she could. She thought someone yelled at her at one point, but she kept her eyes focused straight ahead, her feet moving, and her mouth tight.

* * *

Manek crouched down in a small hole surrounded by plush white snow, remembering the time he was stuck in a similar situation, waiting for Mr. Pilat to come and tell him it was safe. Bronca had rushed out to him and her husband to warn them German soldiers had taken Mamusia and Zosia away. Bronca swore Mamusia would want Manek to stay hidden until it was safe. In an authoritative tone, she told him to go behind the barn and hide. She would find him when it was safe.

The problem was, he hadn't been safe in six years.

He was beginning to wonder if he, Mamusia and Zosia were the only Jews left in the whole wide world.

Closing his eyes, he tried to remember how he made the time pass the day so long ago in the field, waiting for Mr. Pilat. One heartbeat, he seemed to recall. Two heartbeats. Of course, when they were in the ghetto, they had gotten used to counting heartbeats as a way to remind Mamusia they were safe.

Mamusia.

He hoped she was with Zosia. He didn't think he would mind whatever they did to him. He just didn't want them to scare his sister. She had so little joy in her life, she didn't deserve to have anything bad happen to her. She was a very good sister.

It was very cold. He could not stop shaking. He became very tired, and began to close his eyes. Funny how the more tired he got, the less cold it felt outside.

"Maryan. Maryan."

Scowling, he huddled down farther. At some point it must have started to snow. *Funny. Didn't bother him at all.* He was quite warm. "Maryan. Maryan." Manek wondered why Bronca was walking around and yelling. Didn't she know it was time to sleep?

The next time he opened his eyes, he was not sure where he was. The kitchen perhaps. He was swaddled in a wool blanket, lying on the shelf over the fire that kept the room warm. His clothes felt as if they had been frozen and were thawing out. He was just so cold, he could not stop shaking and shivering. Bronca stood over him, trying to feed him something. She had a nice, gentle smile. She wasn't as pretty as his Mamusia, but she made very good borscht and her husband had told him that a woman who cooks was much better than a beautiful one. Manek had thought to himself it would be better to find a woman who could cook and was beautiful ... but as long as she could make that bacon stuff like Mamusia did that time, he would not mind. What was she putting near his mouth now? Was it hot tea? Soup? It really did not matter, as long as it was warm. He tried to take a few sips, and then slipped back into the blissful darkness of sleep.

He kept drifting in and out of consciousness. He knew Bronca had changed him out of his soaked clothes, for he heard her mutter when she changed his pants, "So you really are Jewish." He didn't feel afraid. He just felt as if someone had emptied out his insides and filled him with straw. He couldn't seem to move his body much at all, and his feet were just numb extensions from his hips. Bronca finally managed to get him to swallow some of her delicious borscht.

He knew he was very sick. All he could do was sleep, swallow whatever Bronca poured down his throat, and cough. The cough was so bad it made his body quiver beyond his control. Manek knew he was sick, for he didn't even have the energy to be afraid for his family. His dreams were complicated and mean. He kept seeing Zosia scared and alone without her big brother to protect her. His Mamusia was dead, laid out in the snow where no one could see her. He kept seeing himself running through packed streets as he experienced in the ghetto, desperately searching for them, but no one would help. No one had heard of them.

They disappeared and all that was left was Manek's plaintive cries.

The next morning when he woke, he went up to Bronca and asked where his Mamusia had gone.

"She had to go away somewhere with Zosia, but she should be back soon. Don't worry, everything will be fine. Here, eat some breakfast so that you can get your strength back."

Manek was comforted by the woman's words, but did not feel like eating much. His whole body hurt. Finally, late in the afternoon, the door opened. Sala and Zosia walked in, and Bronca's sigh of relief could be heard in the next room. Manek rushed over to them.

"Where were you? Where did you go?"

Sala bent down to her son and gave him a big hug. "Oh, nothing important, we just had to go visit someone. Don't worry about it, I will tell you all about it later." She felt his head and realized he was feverish. "You do not seem to be feeling well, Maryan. Tell me what hurts."

Manek started to speak, but the coughing fit that overtook him did not allow him to get any words out. Finally, when he could catch a breath, he looked her in the eyes, "I am fine now that we are together again."

CHAPTER TWENTY-FIVE

Winter 1945

The thunder started the next day. This was not a storm but the ear-splitting booms of the artillery fire and cannons which had made up the soundtrack of the long occupation by German forces. Yet this time Sala and Bronca both realized that something big must be happening. They had heard talk that the front was getting closer, that the Germans were retreating. But Sala had learned a long time ago to never hope. That only led to disappointments.

The next change they recognized was the refugees who had once streamed down the roads had slowed to a trickle. They no longer saw big trucks and jeeps with German officers rushing to and fro.

She was working with Zosia in the kitchen. With the number of people the couple had taken in, someone always had to be in the kitchen to keep the never ending line of stomachs filled.

"What is different?"

Zosia shrugged as she worked on the dough she was braiding into bread.

"I can't put my finger on it."

Bronca came bursting through the door. "I see soldiers coming, but they don't look German."

Then Sala realized she could no longer hear the sound of fighting. They'd lived with the echoing booms for so long, she hadn't even noticed when they went away.

How could such a storm as war end and no one marked it?

"What does this mean?"

"I think we are liberated," Bronca grabbed Zosia, threw her up in the air, and spun the little girl around until she giggled.

Sala did not wish to dampen their fun, but it had been too long since she had anything to celebrate. "We must wait and see who comes."

A few hours later, three soldiers banged on the door. The other refugees had congregated in the main room of the house, all of them jumping at the slightest noise from outside. By the time the soldiers came, they were almost relieved from not having to wait anymore. Bronca's husband let them in. They looked around at the anxious faces staring back at them and began to speak rapidly to the group.

"What are they saying?"

"I don't know," Sala answered Manek. "Maybe they speak Russian."

One of the soldiers heard what she said. Addressing her, he spoke very slowly in badly broken Polish. "You are free."

This finally made their point, and the small group broke out into cheers. One of them even grabbed one of the soldiers and hugged him. Bronca's husband brought out some homemade vodka. This apparently was one item that needed no translation. The Russians were happy to enjoy the celebration with the Polish refugees.

Sala realized the Russian who could speak their language somewhat was trying to get their attention. "Germans? We look for them. Have you seen Germans?"

"No," everyone quickly swore.

This seemed to be what they needed to know, and they left. Everyone broke off into their own groups as they tried to decide what they would do next. Sala took Manek and Zosia with her to their room.

"Can it really be true? Can we be free, Mamusia? Is this possible? The war has ended?"

"I hope so, Manek."

"Where do we go now?"

"I do not know, daughter."

"Bronca is nice," Zosia said.

"She is. We will wait for a while to make sure what they said is true. They were Russian soldiers. We do not know if they are honest."

Each day brought more soldiers to their door, and always they had the same exchange. They were free and did they know where the Germans were. Then the questions changed. "Are there Jews here?"

Sala froze. She wanted to scream from the rooftop that she was Jewish. Yet years of being on the run, being raised with her parents' nightmares from World War I had taught her well. *Why would they want to know that? Are they killing us, too? Would this hatred of her people ever stop?* She knew Manek thought they were the last Jews left, but they would never survive unless she continued to be prudent. So she answered without the slightest tremor. "No Jews that I know of."

Bronca agreed with her.

"You have a lot of people gathered in this house. Are you all from here?"

"No," one of the refugees answered.

"We are from many villages," Sala said. "Little places like Brzostek."

"Oh," he waved. "You can go back there. It's safe now. Everything in that direction has been cleared. I wouldn't go the opposite way, though. There are still many Germans fighting rearguard actions."

The kitchen emptied out as everyone broke up to review this latest information. Bronca waited until they were alone to ask, "Why did you not tell them the truth? They are Russian."

"If I had told the truth and their intentions were good, I would have to face the village people next. That would make them distrust you and your priest. If their intentions were bad, there is no place left for us to run."

"You couldn't win either way." Bronca nodded. "I understand."

The next day they left for home. Sala gave the kind couple the largest jewel she had cached in her coat. She embraced them both, thanking them for all of the help and protection for so many months. It was still winter, and the cold was a bitter mistress, but Sala wanted to go back home as fast as she could. She still had their documents proving all that Israel owned before the war. She had the feeling they had to make sure to claim what they owned before the Russians or someone else decided to do it for them.

Bronca and her husband were worried for them. Sala had told them about the Volkdeutsche who were given her house. She still had faith that Antony Pilat had looked out for the farm, even though it had been years since they saw him.

"But, Mamusia," Zosia said. "Why must we leave Bronca and her husband?"

"We are free, my child. You can go back to being Zosia again. Manek shall take his name back, and I will no longer be called Francizka. We are Jews and we are alive. We must make sure that everyone understands the Schonwetters survived, and we are ready to reclaim our family's legacy."

Sala didn't share with her children she also had to see if there was any possibility their father had survived. If he was alive, she knew he would return to Brzostek. So they must as well.

In spite of the frigid conditions they walked all the way home. Bronca sent them with packs of food and warm sweaters to wear, which helped. They kept moving, it felt like weeks as they made their way through snow and gale force winds, determined to make it to the home she barely remembered and she was sure was little more than a dream for Manek and Zosia. Whenever she saw trucks or jeeps coming, she would have the children hide in the bushes. She was not comfortable even being asked if they needed a ride.

As they came at last to the house where she had been married, given birth to her children in and was prepared to die by her husband's side, Sala almost wept at the sight. It was destroyed. A shell must have gone off track and landed on the house. It was empty, so at least she didn't have to fight the hated Volksdeutsche for the home that belonged to her and the children. The windows were all shattered, and the debris of glass and wood shards were scattered everywhere. Someone had looted the interior.

All of their possessions were gone.

The only accommodations she could find, out of the wind and snow, was in the basement. Israel had set up a room for the occasional farm workers he hired. It had no windows, and was in the center of the house so there was some insulation. Once they used the scattered debris to build up a fire, she gave the children their instructions. They scavenged through the remains of the house and made a pile of their "booty" in the small room, which was the only place she could offer them as a home now.

Once she realized they had pots and pans, she just needed food to cook.

Remembering Israel's promise to stockpile some food, Sala left her little ones by the fire to warm up. The caches inside the house were empty. The one in the second barn, however, contained a pile of frozen and badly damaged potatoes. She shredded the potatoes up as best she could with nothing but the knife she'd been given by Bronca's husband and made them potato pancakes.

The next day, she and Manek went back to searching the farm for any leftover stores of food. When she found a bin of wheat, she wanted to cheer. "Mamusia, the mill must be closed. What are we to do with the grain?"

"You and I, my son, are going to grind it by hand. Just like my mama did when I was your age."

Together, she and the children managed to make a rustic, unleavened bread with their hand-ground flour. Such crude conditions were not the dream return she had used to keep herself sane during the years of running and hiding, but they were full and warm. They couldn't ask for more. Though she knew they would never complain, not even Zosia. She kept them all inside the house for almost two weeks, living off the stores from so long ago. If Manek hadn't kept pestering her with questions, she probably would have stayed for months, but her little boy was not to be denied.

The children stayed at the house while she ventured into the village. Before long she realized her worst fears had come true. Even though the Germans had fled the area, their race-based hatred had tainted many of the Polish inhabitants. She heard people talking about Jews who returned to claim their property, only to be killed by those they had once called friend and neighbor.

Sala wasn't recognized. Years of hardship and being on the run had changed her looks drastically. Though she was standing across from people she had known for years, not one of them knew her. She mingled in the marketplace, eyeing the canned goods and small displays of flour with surprise.

Brzostek was once a place where food was as plentiful as people's smiles.

No more. The war had killed her village's spirit.

Her purchases were small. She had no desire to draw any unneeded attention to them. When she was walking away, with her head bowed down, she froze at the sight before her. She would recognize those shoes anywhere. She quickly looked up and was stunned to see the man wearing them, Heniek. At first he did not realize who was standing only a few feet away.

Sala followed him through the village, determined to confront him when he was alone.

"Heniek."

He whirled around and stared. "Sala?" Without hesitation, he ran to her, stopping short when he realized she was not as happy to see him as he was her.

"Why are you wearing my husband's shoes?"

She pointed at the shiny leather and unique stitching of shoes she had ordered specially for Israel the year before the war broke out. She had to send all the way to Warsaw for them. Israel had only worn them for shul and his most important meetings. "Those are Israel's. Where did you get them?"

Her voice was getting shrill as her breath came in pants. Heniek guided her to a bench and together they sat in the weak sunshine. He hesitantly began his tale:

"The night they took Israel, I was at the station house. It was my night to stand guard at the jail cell. When I saw them bring Israel in, I knew it was not good. When the Germans left for the night, I went in and opened the cell where Israel was kept. I told him to go."

Sala closed her eyes as she pictured Israel inside her mind. He would have been confused. He would have been hopeful. "What did he do?"

"I do not know." Heniek shook his head. "All I am sure of was he left only for a little while. When he returned, I was shocked and demanded he escape. I begged him. Told him to run, to go find his family. Your husband, Sala, he would not."

"No. He wouldn't." A small sob escaped her lips before she could swallow it down.

"Israel told me he would never be able to live with himself if even one person suffered on his behalf. He was prepared to die for his faith. He was fine with dying for his people. He could not live, knowing someone else had died, or been hurt in his place. He only asked of me one request." Heniek paused and composed himself. "He made me promise him that we would help you and the children survive. He told me that you were a person that could endure the terrible odds."

Her sobs broke free and she cried for a long time beside Heniek. He sat silently, allowing her the time to grieve. When she finally recovered some control over her emotions, she encouraged him.

"Tell me the rest. Please, I beg you. I need to know it all."

"I was part of the forced work detail for the Germans."

Sala tried to smile. "I thought they just did that to the Jews."

"No. They ended up commandeering us all. I was taken with a group of men deep in the forest. We were told to dig a pit. The Germans brought all of the Jews from Brzostek. Both the ones who lived here still and the ones they brought in from elsewhere. They lined them at the edge of the pit and ..."

"They shot them in the head." She had seen this horror in the ghetto, in the woods, and heard others speak of such atrocities every day at Bronca's.

"Yes, ma'am. When they were done, the Germans told us to take what we wanted from the bodies and fill in the mass grave. I wasn't going to take anything. Then I saw your husband and his shiny shoes. I took them to remind myself what an honor it is to walk in the footsteps of someone so courageous and honorable. I am deeply sorry for your loss. If you would like them back—"

Sala stopped Heniek as he reached down to pull off the shoes. "No." He looked doubtfully at her, so she shook her head again. "No. You keep them. Thank you for telling me, though. I am grateful to know the truth. And thank you for all that you and Antony have done for us."

"Sala, is there something I can do for you now? Please? I would really like to know I did something more for you."

"Is your father-in-law still alive?"

"He is."

"Tell him that I am at the house with Manek and Zosia. Tell him I am ready to deliver on my promise." Sala gathered her packages and slowly made her way back to the children. She thought about the silly stories they used to entertain each other during the long hours of hiding. She finally had one to tell them, though this time the hero was their own father, and the grand adventure he went on was to protect his honor and dignity.

The ending was not one she would have written. Only fairy tales end in happily ever after. What would be her ending? What would be her children's? Only time would tell, but hopefully the ending of this chapter would give them comfort as they finished writing the rest of the story.

EPILOGUE

by Ann Arnold

In the end, staying together was the key that allowed my grandmother, aunt and father to survive the Holocaust during World War II in Poland. In the end they would find freedom. Freedom to grow up. Freedom to believe in their faith. Freedom for my Aunt and Father to find love and have children of their own.

After giving Antony Pilat the house she promised him, Sala, Manek, and Zosia moved to Tarnow, the nearest big city to the village of Brzostek. There they were able to get help from the UNAID council. They also found protection in the greater community of surviving Jews, for, unlike my father's fears, they were not the only Jews left. Manek had gotten pneumonia the second time he almost froze to death while hiding outside Bronca's house. This led to tuberculosis, and when they got to Tarnow, he was sent for a couple of months to a hospital for treatment.

When the first Jewish high holidays came around, Sala Schonwetter went to synagogue. Sometime during the blowing of the ram's horn, Sala found her way back to God, and perhaps, in her own way, found a way to forgive herself for having to deny who and what she was so many times in order to keep her family alive. She kept Kosher the rest of her life, and never tasted bacon again.

Once a week, my grandmother would take a bus to Brzostek on Wednesdays, to visit the farmer's market, where she would buy meat, eggs and other staples. The prices were much cheaper there. She was also able to connect with her family in America. She had three sisters and a brother that had left Poland long before the war started. After the cease fire they wrote a letter to Brzostek, desperately looking for survivors. She received their letter and was able to reconnect with the only family members she had left.

The trips to Brzostek also allowed her to begin selling off her land. She had no money, and her only assets were her home and property. After giving Antony one of the houses she owned and some land, she then began slowly selling off parts of the rest of the vast farmland. Eventually, she sold her old house, since it was no longer her home. The family that bought the house still own it today. She was able to make a little money this way. In order to raise further sums, Sala began to buy and sell American dollars on the black market. She would always find a way to support her children. In Tarnow, she soon met up with some other familiar faces, Romek and Fish.

Romek never really gave up his rowdy, randy, and thieving ways. Although it helped him survive the war, he eventually got himself in trouble and ended up in jail. He escaped once but was recaptured and eventually died in prison.

As for Fish, he had found only one survivor in his own family, despite searching far and wide. Solomon Katzbach was his brother-in-law, the only one to survive through the war. Solomon and Sala healed each other of their grief, and they were eventually married in 1947. Since America closed its borders to Polish refugees due to the Russian influence, they managed to emigrate to Israel in 1957, where Sala hoped they would be safe. They were together until the day he died in 1968. Sala never remarried again.

Manek, my father, still had wandering feet, though, and eventually made his way to America.

Fish confessed finally what had happened the night of the raid from the police that cost Ignash his life. Ignash had been wounded, and they tried to carry him to safety. The police were relentless, though. Afraid of being caught, recognizing Ignash was mortally wounded, Romek put him out of his misery.

As I grew up, I never truly considered the dramatic turn my father's childhood had taken. Going from the cherished son of a successful landowner to a hunted boy who was forced to live in a hole in the floor of a pig sty, is a journey that overwhelms my imagination, so I can't imagine how someone who doesn't know him personally might feel.

Only after I had children myself did I understand parts of the story all the way down in my soul. My grandmother's courage, strength and perseverance will always stand as an example of the superhero-like qualities that can be found in a mother's love. She swore to her husband she would keep them together. She kept her word. In Poland, where most Jews did not live through the war, and many died in the turmoil and violence that followed the war, Sala Schonwetter not only got both of their children through it, she lived to see her grandchildren and great-grandchildren grow up both in the country of the free and the brave and the country promised to her people by God.

I believe Manek took deeply to heart the advice given to him in the forest by Fish and Romek and by Bronca's husband. He found a woman who was both beautiful and could make one amazing bowl of borscht. My mother is all of those things and more.

He did not return to Poland again until 1993. My father, mother, sister and I went on a family trip. It was a moving experience to witness firsthand the places that I had heard so much about. But as special as that trip was, our next trip to Poland in 2009 was life-changing.

My whole life, I had been searching for a meaning, for someone to give me a reason as to why this happened. It wasn't fair! I was deprived of my family, and more important, my father and aunt were deprived of the innocence of childhood, almost deprived of a childhood at all. I realize there is no answer, but in the end there is a lesson. No matter how dark things may seem, there will always be light. Sala was able to see the light, and in 2009, so were we.

A few years before, Jonathan Weber, a religious studies professor in England whose family immigrated to England from Brzostek in the late 1800s, petitioned the state of Poland, the town, and the head of the Rabbinical College of Rabbis to reinstate the Jewish cemetery in Brzostek. After many years the head rabbi of Poland agreed, and a massive undertaking was begun. The cemetery was destroyed in 1942 and therefore prior to June 2009 all had that remained was an empty lot of land. Professor Weber took it upon himself to reach out to the mayor and the priest of Brzostek to help him rebuild a sacred site.

Amazingly, we found out, the entire community got behind this project. When the town heard about what was happening, the people of Brzostek realized its importance and rallied to help, finding headstones that had been used for masonry work or finding them in junkyards. By the time the cemetery was ready to be unveiled, the people of Brzostek had found over thirty original headstones from the cemetery. Amazingly, one of the matzevahs (head stones) that was returned was that of my great-grandfather, Fischel Schonwetter.

The day of the opening was a day I will never forget. None of us knew what to expect. Honestly, we were thinking it would be a nice little ceremony, with a few dozen people.

First, we congregated at Town Hall, which also housed the jail, the very same one my grandfather refused to escape from, to unveil a memorial plaque that was hung outside the building. This ceremony was attended by about 20 foreigners that had some connection to the cemetery, along with about 30 townspeople, including the mayor and local priest. We were surprised, at this point, that so many local people had come out, showing they cared.

The plaque reads:

IN MEMORY OF THE JEWISH COMMUNITY OF BRZOSTEK ITS RABBIS, TEACHERS, SHOPKEEPERS AND ARTISANS AND ALL FAMILIES AND IN MEMORY OF 500 JEWISH MEN, WOMEN AND CHILDREN OF BRZOSTEK MURDERED IN 1942 IN THE PODZAMCZE FOREST, IN THE BEZEC DEATH CAMP AND OTHER UNKOWN PLACES.

After this small ceremony, we walked five minutes down the road. As we turned the final corner, I was shocked by what I saw.

Hundreds of people from the community, both young and old, came to attend and witness what, to me, was a very emotional and historic moment. All of us were speechless. We could not fathom that so many townspeople had taken the time on this morning to come and witness this event. Tents and chairs were set up for people to sit on, but there was not enough for everyone. The first few rows had been left empty for the "VIP's"—how funny that my father and his sister were now being welcomed as a VIP. The turn of events was totally unbelievable.

Speeches were made by many, including my father and aunt. During my father's speech, he recounted some of the stories you have just read. I heard people behind me that made comments, as they remembered the family names of some of the people that had saved my father. Zosia Dziedzic, whose family saved so many Jews, including my family, attended the ceremony. My father does not cry, ever, but he got choked up when he started to talk about his mother. The sun was shining and there was not a cloud in the sky. It was as if my grandparents were looking down on us from above, with the best view of all.

After the speeches, prayers and blessings were recited, the shofar was blown and we proceeded to the gates of the cemetery. We had erected a tombstone in memory of my grandfather, here in this cemetery.

In the Jewish religion, when someone dies, the family recites a prayer (like a blessing for the dead) called Kaddish. It meant the world to me to hear Kaddish being said for my grandfather, and to know that he had received a final place of rest at last. Astoundingly enough, three years later the mass grave he was killed in was uncovered. An anonymous party marked it with an etched tombstone—another remarkable example of true goodness.

I approached the mayor after the service and thanked him for giving my grandfather a final resting place and providing me with a place that I can bring my children. I will never forget his response: "You don't need to thank me. It was the right thing to do, the only thing to do." I hate to admit that I kept thinking, these people are really doing this for what? What are they getting out of it?

Following this very emotional afternoon, the crowd left the cemetery and was invited to attend an assembly put together by the students of the high school. They had buses for all of us visitors to take us the short distance. When we got to the school, the site was astounding.

The children and their families had used the internet to research authentic Jewish recipes and cooked homemade Jewish and Polish dishes for us, in a buffet that was almost 20 feet long. They also prepared kosher meals for those that were observant. After we indulged in some delicious food, we sat down to hear the concert that they had prepared. These Polish children had learned and sang Hebrew Jewish songs, like "Shalom Aleichem" and "Hava Nagila," and according to my aunt, who lives in Israel, they sang it better than most Israelis. We learned that the school has now incorporated into their high school curriculum Jewish studies, and Professor Weber established an annual scholarship for students. You have to remember, not one Jewish person has lived in this town since 1942. To know that the future generations will learn about the real history of their town, their country and the many people that no longer live there makes me feel that there is still hope and that the hell that my father, aunt, grandmother and millions of other Jews experienced will not be forgotten.

As Jews we know how important and fragile our heritage is, and as children of holocaust survivors, we cannot help but feel cheated for not having the opportunity to know our lost family. But to know that others understand this as well has truly restored my faith in humankind. We always preach, "Never Forget," and it is heartwarming to know that our ancestral community takes this very seriously. I hope we can all learn from their example. In a way I see this as closure for my father, and I hope that it can be the beginning of a compassionate and understanding journey that other towns and communities will venture upon.

This book was written for my own great grandchildren and all those grandchildren who were not as blessed as I was to hear these kinds of stories from Sala's lips. I hope you find your own sense of honor as my grandfather did when he refused to continue his life at the cost of another. I pray you are like Manek and Zosia, and have a mother who has the strength, will and ingenuity of Sala.

And if you don't have one, I hope you are one to another.

When I was younger, I used to write a little poetry. I recently looked back at some of the works I had done, and found this piece I wrote during my teenage years. I hope you all take it to heart and share this story:

Those of you who feel you are not affected, are affected the most

Those of you who feel it did not happen to you, will experience it the most

Those of you who don't want to remember, will have the most terrifying nightmares

Those of you who think it never happened, will live through it again.

They survived because they stayed TOGETHER. On the bottom row, starting from left to right, is Zosia Schonwetter, Romek, Sala Schonwetter, Manek Schonwetter and Fish. Right above Sala in the middle, with light hair, is Zosia Dziedzic, the woman who helped, along with her family, to save so many.

From Left to Right – Zosia Schonwetter, Sala Schonwetter, Solomon Katzbach, Manek Schonwetter – Post War in Tarnow

Manek and Zosia Schonwetter 1937

Manek and Zosia Schonwetter, Poland 2009

ANN S. ARNOLD

 I never intended on being a writer. I realize how controversial that statement is, but it's true. The only footsteps I ever wanted to follow was my father, Mark Schonwetter's, right into the jewelry business. Writing seemed far beyond my scope of experience, though I have always loved to read, and my secret desire was to do just this. We have entered the time period where the true witnesses and victims of the Holocaust are dying, so we, as a society, are losing a vital source of truth. My family's experience during the war, the fortitude of my grandmother Sala and the strength of my father, is a treasured legacy. I was blessed to be given this legacy, and learn its lessons throughout my formative years. Now I want to share it with the world.